Current
CONTROVERSIES

Homelessness and Street Crime

Other Books in the Current Controversies Series

Current
CONTROVERSIES

Homelessness and Street Crime

Pete Schauer, Book Editor

GREENHAVEN
PUBLISHING

Published in 2018 by Greenhaven Publishing, LLC
353 3rd Avenue, Suite 255, New York, NY 10010

Articles in Greenhaven Publishing anthologies are often edited for length to meet page
requirements. In addition, original titles of these works are changed to clearly present
the main thesis and to explicitly indicate the author's opinion. Every effort is made to
ensure that Greenhaven Publishing accurately reflects the original intent of the authors.
Every effort has been made to trace the owners of the copyrighted material.

Cover image: Rebecca Vale/Alamy Stock Photo

Library of Congress Cataloging-in-Publication Data

Names: Schauer, Pete, editor.
Title: Homelessness and street crime / edited by Pete Schauer.
Description: New York : Greenhaven Publishing, 2018. | Series: Current
  controversies | Includes bibliographical references and index. | Audience: Grades 9-12.
Identifiers: LCCN ISBN 9781534500952 (library bound) | ISBN 9781534500938
  (pbk.)
Subjects: LCSH: Homelessness--United States--Juvenile literature. | Homeless
  persons--United States--Juvenile literature. | Crime--United States--Juvenile
  literature.
Classification: LCC HV4505.H65528 2018 | DDC 362.5?920973--dc23

Manufactured in the United States of America

Website: http://greenhavenpublishing.com

Contents

Chapter 1: Does Being Homeless Lead to a Life of Street Crime?

Stephen Baron
How a young individual is raised plays an important role on homeless youth, who often adapt to life on the streets by committing crimes such as drug dealing and robbery in order to stay alive.

Yes: Being Homeless Leads to a Life of Street Crime

National Network for Youth
Mental health issues, substance abuse, and trouble in school are some of the most popular factors that enhance the odds of a young person becoming homeless.

John Hagan and Bill McCarthy
Data suggests that families with backgrounds of violence and crime are more likely to produce a child who will commit a crime and be charged by police than families who don't have a history of violence or crime.

Best MSW Programs
There's a direct correlation between mental illness and homelessness, with 385,000 homeless people in the US suffering from untreated schizophrenia or manic depression, and a number of them will end up in prison.

Yes: We Have a Responsibility to Help the Homeless

Department for Communities and Local Government
The government has a responsibility to both the homeless and the
non-homeless to develop committees and create plans to put an end
to homelessness.

Government of Western Australia
Western Australia has developed a State Plan that brings government
agencies and community organizations together to create a strategy
to bring homelessness to an end.

Bill & Melinda Gates Foundation
Bill Gates, former CEO of Microsoft, and his wife, Melinda, are
helping to provide transitional housing in Washington State through
the Sound Families Initiative.

No: We Do Not Have a Responsibility to Help the Homeless

Dr. Tracy Miller
Despite efforts in some locations to provide free housing or other
forms of shelter, the number of homeless increased. The lack of
evidence to support that government-funded shelter has helped
reduce homelessness doesn't help the argument that we need to do
more for the homeless.

Kylyssa Shay
People think that only the lower class can fall victim to homelessness,
but when examining all of the reasons why people end up homeless,
the middle and upper classes aren't exempt from living on the street.

Natalia
Natalia, a Nigerian-born woman with wealthy parents, tells her story
as to how she ended up homeless in a new country. This personal
narrative proves that almost anyone can end up homeless.

Chapter 4: Would Ending Homelessness Help Reduce Street Crime?

Foreword

Controversy is a word that has an undeniably unpleasant connotation. It carries a definite negative charge. Controversy can spoil family gatherings, spread a chill around classroom and campus discussion, inflame public discourse, open raw civic wounds, and lead to the ouster of public officials. We often feel that controversy is almost akin to bad manners, a rude and shocking eruption of that which must not be spoken or thought of in polite, tightly guarded society. To avoid controversy, to quell controversy, is often seen as a public good, a victory for etiquette, perhaps even a moral or ethical imperative.

Yet the studious, deliberate avoidance of controversy is also a whitewashing, a denial, a death threat to democracy. It is a false sterilizing and sanitizing and superficial ordering of the messy, ragged, chaotic, at times ugly processes by which a healthy democracy identifies and confronts challenges, engages in passionate debate about appropriate approaches and solutions, and arrives at something like a consensus and a broadly accepted and supported way forward. Controversy is the megaphone, the speaker's corner, the public square through which the citizenry finds and uses its voice. Controversy is the life's blood of our democracy and absolutely essential to the vibrant health of our society.

Our present age is certainly no stranger to controversy. We are consumed by fierce debates about technology, privacy, political correctness, poverty, violence, crime and policing, guns, immigration, civil and human rights, terrorism, militarism, environmental protection, and gender and racial equality. Loudly competing voices are raised every day, shouting opposing opinions, putting forth competing agendas, and summoning starkly different visions of a utopian or dystopian future. Often these voices attempt to shout the others down; there is precious little listening and considering among the cacophonous din. Yet listening and

considering, too, are essential to the health of a democracy. If controversy is democracy's lusty lifeblood, respectful listening and careful thought are its higher faculties, its brain, its conscience.

Current Controversies does not shy away from or attempt to hush the loudly competing voices. It seeks to provide readers with as wide and representative as possible a range of articulate voices on any given controversy of the day, separates each one out to allow it to be heard clearly and fairly, and encourages careful listening to each of these well-crafted, thoughtfully expressed opinions, supplied by some of today's leading academics, thinkers, analysts, politicians, policy makers, economists, activists, change agents, and advocates. Only after listening to a wide range of opinions on an issue, evaluating the strengths and weaknesses of each argument, assessing how well the facts and available evidence mesh with the stated opinions and conclusions, and thoughtfully and critically examining one's own beliefs and conscience can the reader begin to arrive at his or her own conclusions and articulate his or her own stance on the spotlighted controversy.

This process is facilitated and supported in each Current Controversies volume by an introduction and chapter overviews that provide readers with the essential context they need to begin engaging with the spotlighted controversies, with the debates surrounding them, and with their own perhaps shifting or nascent opinions on them. Chapters are organized around several key questions that are answered with diverse opinions representing all points on the political spectrum. In its content, organization, and methodology, readers are encouraged to determine the authors' point of view and purpose, interrogate and analyze the various arguments and their rhetoric and structure, evaluate the arguments' strengths and weaknesses, test their claims against available facts and evidence, judge the validity of the reasoning, and bring into clearer, sharper focus the reader's own beliefs and conclusions and how they may differ from or align with those in the collection or those of classmates.

Research has shown that reading comprehension skills improve dramatically when students are provided with compelling, intriguing, and relevant "discussable" texts. The subject matter of these collections could not be more compelling, intriguing, or urgently relevant to today's students and the world they are poised to inherit. The anthologized articles also provide the basis for stimulating, lively, and passionate classroom debates. Students who are compelled to anticipate objections to their own argument and identify the flaws in those of an opponent read more carefully, think more critically, and steep themselves in relevant context, facts, and information more thoroughly. In short, using discussable text of the kind provided by every single volume in the Current Controversies series encourages close reading, facilitates reading comprehension, fosters research, strengthens critical thinking, and greatly enlivens and energizes classroom discussion and participation. The entire learning process is deepened, extended, and strengthened.

If we are to foster a knowledgeable, responsible, active, and engaged citizenry, we must provide readers with the intellectual, interpretive, and critical-thinking tools and experience necessary to make sense of the world around them and of the all-important debates and arguments that inform it. We must encourage them not to run away from or attempt to quell controversy but to embrace it in a responsible, conscientious, and thoughtful way, to sharpen and strengthen their own informed opinions by listening to and critically analyzing those of others. This series encourages respectful engagement with and analysis of current controversies and competing opinions and fosters a resulting increase in the strength and rigor of one's own opinions and stances. As such, it helps readers assume their rightful place in the public square and provides them with the skills necessary to uphold their awesome responsibility—guaranteeing the continued and future health of a vital, vibrant, and free democracy.

Introduction

> *"What led up to my becoming*
> *homeless was that I was laid off from*
> *a job which I had for several years*
> *and… my house burned down…*
> *What I realized was that my skills*
> *had become less relevant and I wasn't*
> *all that employable… I had 20th*
> *century work skills…"*
>
> *–John Harrison,*
> *Formerly Homeless Person*

If you live in or have visited a major city, chances are you have passed by a homeless person on the street, and that brief moment likely struck an emotion inside of you. Whether it was anger, sadness, remorse, sympathy, or any other type of emotion, you felt something and knew that this was not the type of life that you would want for you and your family. Unfortunately, though, not everyone is afforded the luxury of having four walls and a roof around them each day. According to the National Alliance to End Homelessness, there are more than 633,000 people who are homeless on any given night in the United States.

We see the word "homeless" and think we understand what it means, but having a place to call home day in and day out is something that we take for granted, especially when you consider the types of people who are being left without a home. Of those 633,000+ people, more than 22% are children and 13% are veterans who served their country to help keep us safe, while more than

40% are people who are unable to work due to disability, according to Front Steps.

On the flip side, criminals and substance abusers who have broken the law are also part of the more than half a million homeless each night, and this feeds into the stereotype—by some people—that the homeless are criminals and nothing more. In fact, some cities across the U.S. have essentially made it illegal to be homeless, handing out fines to people who are "camping," sleeping in public, or even sleeping in a car. Additionally, food sharing, or sharing food with homeless people, has been outlawed in some U.S. cities under the assumption that free food services would attract more homeless people to a certain area, or that free food would encourage people to remain homeless.

When you take the time to actually consider who our homeless are in the United States, the information can be staggering, especially when you consider that there are war veterans coming home from overseas who are not being supported and given the care and support that they deserve and need. And while there are the homeless who have broken the law and have been convicted of a crime, there are others who simply fell on hard times due to a break up with a spouse, loss of a loved one, or loss of a job, and were never able to recover, especially in this day and age where the cost of living only continues to increase.

With all of this said, this raises the question of whether or not we have a responsibility to help those that are homeless, and more importantly, if we do, what exactly are we—the people and our government—doing to help them? While some local governments and city officials have made an effort to penalize the homeless, others have taken strides to provide free public housing and food for the homeless. For example, the city of Sarasota, Florida has developed an action plan to help the homeless by hiring a city coordinator to focus solely on improving the homeless situation within Sarasota, organizing and developing a housing program, and providing mental health facilities, to name a few things. Many other cities around the country have adopted this type of thinking,

putting conscious effort and funds into providing the homeless with resources to survive and better their quality of life. But at the end of the day, it's difficult to break the public perception by those who see all homeless people as criminals. The issues surrounding the debate are examined and argued by authoritative voices on the topic in *Current Controversies: Homelessness and Street Crime*.

Does Being Homeless Lead to a Life of Street Crime?

Overview: The Homeless Often Have to Commit Petty Crimes in Order to Survive

Stephen Baron

A Sociology professor at Queen's University at Kingston in Ontario, Canada, Stephen Baron's main focus of research is on the link between street youth and criminal behavior.

Introduction

Research on homeless street youth in Canada suggests that these young people are heavily "at risk" of becoming involved in criminal activities (Baron, 1995; Gaetz, 2004; Hagan & McCarthy, 1997). The factors that contribute to why and how street youth come to engage in illegal activities are many and often complex. In the following chapter I summarize my research over the past two decades, as well as draw on the work of other Canadian researchers, to explore a range of factors that explain why street youth become involved in property crime, drug dealing, and violence. I begin with a short overview of the extent of street youth's participation in crime and then move to outlining the background factors in these young people's lives that affect the way they behave on the street. I then explore how homelessness and unemployment influence participation in a range of crimes. The key here is understanding not only how severe poverty can lead to offending, but also how individual perceptions of poverty can shape these youth's responses to their difficult situations. The chapter also details how street peers, street culture, and street lifestyles sway youth's decisions to engage in illegal behaviour. Further, I explore the social-psychological factors that develop in response to adverse circumstances and which contribute to youth's criminal behaviours, as well as youth's responses to potential criminal punishments and their influence

Baron, S. (2013). Why Street Youth Become Involved in Crime. In Gaetz, S., O'Grady, B., Buccieri, K., Karabanow, J., & Marsolais, A. (Eds.), Youth Homelessness in Canada: Implications for Policy and Practice (353-368). Toronto: Canadian Observatory on Homelessness Press.

on criminal choices. I end by reviewing the potential policy implications of the findings.

To What Extent Are Street Youth Involved in Crime?

Research shows that compared to their housed peers, street youth are more likely to be involved in a range of criminal activities (Baron, 1995; Gaetz, 2004; Hagan & McCarthy, 1997; O'Grady et al., 2011; Tanner & Wortley, 2002). For example, I found that male youth living on the street in Edmonton committed almost 1,700 offenses each on average in a year (Baron, 1995). While these numbers are large, it is important to acknowledge that street youth are involved in criminal behaviour to different degrees. Research reveals that a large minority of youth on the street engage in relatively little or no criminal activity (Baron, 1995; Gaetz, 2004; Hagan & McCarthy, 1997; O'Grady et al., 2011). To illustrate, Gaetz (2004) found that 37 percent of street youth in his sample had not engaged in any criminal activity. There are, however, youth who engage in high rates of crime. My work in Edmonton showed that 20 percent of the youth sampled were very high rate offenders committing over 2,000 offenses in the prior year (Baron, 1995).

The types of offenses these youth are involved in vary. For example, in my 1995 study, 20 percent of the total number of offenses committed were property crimes. O'Grady et al., (2011) show that 19 percent of the youth they interviewed in Toronto had stolen something from a person, 22 percent had stolen food, and 20 percent had stolen clothes or shoes. I found youth also stole from cars, broke into houses and buildings, and took motor vehicles.

Most youth who engage in property crimes do so for utilitarian purposes. Gaetz (2004) outlines that 53 percent of the street youth in his study had shoplifted for their own use and 38 percent had stolen something for the purposes of reselling. Generally, youth resort to theft for survival or to help cope with being on the street (Baron, 1995; Gaetz & O'Grady, 2002; O'Grady et al., 2011). Research shows that youth use money gained by theft to buy food or clothes, to secure shelter, or to purchase drugs and alcohol.

The distribution or selling of drugs also contributes to street youth's high number of offenses (Baron, 1995; Gaetz, 2004; McCarthy & Hagan, 1991; O'Grady et al., 2011). In my Edmonton work (1995) selling drugs was the largest contributor to offense rates; the average youth indicated participating in 1,200 transactions (i.e. drug deals) in the past year. Of the 56 percent of youth in the study who reported selling drugs, over a quarter had sold drugs more than 2,000 times. More recent research finds similar patterns. Gaetz (2004) found that 50 percent of his Toronto sample had sold drugs. O'Grady et al., (2011) reported that 36 percent of their sample sold marijuana, 17 percent sold crack cocaine, and 20 percent sold other drugs. Like property offending, youth report they are involved in the drug trade to earn money for survival and 355 LEGAL & JUSTICE ISSUES to support their own substance use (Baron, 1995; Gaetz & O'Grady, 2002).

Finally, street youth are involved in a great deal of violent crime. Youth in my (1995) research reported committing an average of 82 violent crimes per year. Over 58 percent of these violent offenses involved robbery where the youth took money, jewellery and other valuable items from people by force or the threat of force. Violent crimes also include assaults of varying degrees of seriousness, as well as physical altercations (fights) between groups of youth. Gaetz (2004) found that 42 percent of the street youth in his Toronto study had been involved in an assault for reasons other than self-defense in the prior 12 months; and O'Grady et al., (2011) showed that 20 percent of respondents used a weapon while committing a crime.

To summarize, a minority of the street youth population is heavily involved in a range of criminal activities. At the same time many youth on the streets have chosen not to engage in these activities. What does the research tell us about why certain youth are more at risk of offending?

Background Factors and Crime on the Street Research consistently reveals that the path to the street often begins with negative family backgrounds. Hagan and McCarthy (1997) show

that adverse economic circumstances foster psychological and economic stress in homes. This stress hampers parents' ability to care for children and increases the likelihood that inconsistent and coercive methods of discipline will be utilized. Studies show that youth on the streets have often suffered high rates of abuse (Forde et al., 2012; Hagan & McCarthy, 1997; Whitbeck & Hoyt, 1999). Street youth have often experienced physical neglect, including food insecurity (situations in which their homes lack food for regular meals), a lack of clean clothing, and a lack of medical attention (Forde et al., 2012). Their parents often had alcohol and/or drug problems that undermined their ability to care and provide for their children (Forde et al., 2012; Hagan & McCarthy, 1997). Street youth also frequently encountered emotional neglect where support and affection from family members was absent (Forde et al., 2012; Whitbeck & Hoyt, 1999). Many street youth also report having experienced emotional abuse from members of their family; incidences which involved being regularly insulted and hurt over comments directed at them (Forde et al., 2012). Further, many street youth describe high rates of physical abuse, often so serious that victims were left physically damaged (Forde et al., 2012; Hagan & McCarthy, 1997; Whitbeck & Hoyt, 1999). Finally, some youth have encountered sexual abuse (Forde et al., 2012; Hagan & McCarthy, 1997; Whitbeck & Hoyt, 1999).

Criminologists suggest these experiences leave one at greater risk for criminal behaviour (Baron, 2004; Hagan & McCarthy, 1997). Childhood abuse can jeopardize a child's needs, values and/or identity, and is seen as unjust by those who experience it (Agnew, 2006; Baron, 2004). Abuse also serves to weaken youth's emotional attachments to caregivers and undermines the influence of parents and other adults. This lack of attachment means less concern for the wishes and opinions of others leaving one free to commit crime (Baron, 2003a; 2004; Baron et al., 2001). Youth who experience emotional abuse come to view the world as a coercive, hostile environment, leading them to become hostile and aggressive in their interactions with others (Baron, 2003a; 2004; Baron et al.,

2001). Children who experience more physically violent forms of abuse often see aggression as the way to solve problems and adopt values and attitudes that support the use of violence (Baron, 2003a; 2004; Baron et al., 2001). Physical abuse also undermines one's ability to cope with future negative experiences and stresses, and harms the development of compassion and empathy, increasing the likelihood one will victimize others (Baron, 2003a; 2004; Baron et al., 2001). Physical abuse also leads youth to seek out and create violent situations including joining peers who use, support, and encourage violence (Baron, 2003a; 2004; Baron & Hartnagel, 1998). Sexual abuse can result in feelings of betrayal, hostility, and anger, as well as lead to a sense of powerlessness that damages coping abilities. Feelings of guilt, shame and stigmatization leave victims more likely to be drawn to others who are stigmatized, including criminally involved peers (Baron, 2003a; 2004).

Research outlines that certain experiences of abuse tend to be associated with certain forms of offending. In particular, street youth who have suffered physical abuse are at an increased risk of engaging in higher rates of criminal activity when compared to those who have not had these experiences (Baron, 2004; Gaetz & O'Grady, 2002; Hagan & McCarthy, 1997; Whitbeck & Hoyt, 1999). There is a strong link between the experience of physical abuse and violent offending (Baron, 2004; Hagan & McCarthy, 1997), particularly robberies and more serious forms of violence where victims suffer significant injuries (Baron & Hartnagel, 1998). It is unclear if there is a direct link between sexual abuse and the offenses being looked at in this chapter since research has produced support both for and against this link (see Chen et al., 2007; Gaetz & O'Grady, 2002; Hagan & McCarthy, 1997; Tyler & Johnson, 2006; Whitbeck & Hoyt, 1999). While the role of its direct relationship to crime is in dispute, sexual abuse has been found to lead to crime when accompanied by certain other factors. My research shows that youth who have histories of sexual abuse are more involved in violence if they have also acquired and developed values that support the use of violence or associate with peers who support

and use violence (Baron, 2004). As I will show later, the street is an arena where there is support for the use of violence.

Levels of self-esteem also appear to influence how street youth channel their abusive experiences. I (2004) discovered that physical abuse was more likely to lead to violence amongst street youth who, despite the abuse, had higher levels of self-esteem than their street peers. Similarly, youth who had experienced emotional abuse were more likely to be involved in property offenses when they had higher levels of self-esteem. I have argued elsewhere (2004) that self-esteem may allow one to adopt a criminal route to combat repression and assist in bringing a sense of balance back into one's life (see Tittle, 1995). Alternatively, crime may be a method of reaffirming self-esteem that is diminished during the experiences of abuse (see Baumeister et al., 1996).

Homelessness and Crime

Youth who flee their homes for the streets enter an environment that promotes participation in crime. Youth find themselves in need of food, money, and shelter (Hagan & McCarthy, 1997). Criminologists recognize that the experience of homelessness can have a powerful impact on individuals and note its potentially strong link to criminal activities. Becoming homeless is felt to be unjust by those who experience it and threatens an individual's needs, values, goals and/or identities (Agnew, 2006; Baron, 2004). Homelessness also reduces one's contact with the people and institutions of regular society and breaks previous social ties. With no relationships to maintain and little stake in social institutions, people who become homeless have little to lose if convicted of a crime; in sociological terms, social control has little power over them (Agnew, 2006; Baron & Hartnagel, 1997; Hagan & McCarthy, 1997).

Homelessness also provides opportunities for crime. Youth who lack shelter are often forced to spend a significant amount of time in public locations. This public lifestyle brings individuals into contact with tempting property and

human targets for victimization (Baron & Hartnagel, 1997). Homelessness also provides an environment where crime can be learned (Hagan & McCarthy, 1997; McCarthy, 1996). On the street, youth encounter other young people involved in criminal activities. These other offenders are criminal models for those new to the streets and provide training and encouragement for criminal activities (Baron & Hartnagel, 1997; 1998; Hagan & McCarthy, 1997). These peers can facilitate criminal activities that require accomplices and can offer approval for their friends' criminal behaviour. Further, homelessness exposes youth to an alternative culture that values many forms of offending, including property offending, drug dealing, and violence (Baron, 2009a; Baron & Hartnagel, 1997). Many street youth are drawn to this street culture because it reflects and extends some of the lessons learned from abusive backgrounds (Baron, 2009a; Colvin, 2000). Together, youth on the street develop new standards and expectations for behaviour. In this environment the morals and expectations of the broader society are rejected and new ones substituted that allow street youth to more effectively cope with their life situations (Baron, 2006; 2009a; Baron & Hartnagel, 1997). Included in this culture is support for the use of criminal means to overcome financial struggles (Baron, 2006; Baron & Hartnagel, 1997). Street youth are directly educated in this culture through social rewards for criminal behaviour, and social punishments for reluctance to participate, as well as through their observation of other street youth's behaviours (Baron, 2011b; Baron & Hartnagel, 1997). My research consistently reveals that both having values that support criminal behaviour and having criminally involved peers leads to criminal activity on the street (Baron, 2004; 2006; 2008; 2009a). Hagan and McCarthy (1997) show how homelessness increases the chances that youth will become involved in "coaching" relationships where they are taught to engage in theft and drug dealing, offered protection, and helped to sell stolen property and drugs (see also McCarthy et

al., 1998). Through these coaching relationships, street youth undertake more criminal activities than those not engaged in these relationships (Hagan & McCarthy, 1997).

Research reveals that the longer one stays on the streets, the more likely one is to engage in various forms of crime (Baron, 2003b; 2004; Baron & Hartnagel, 1997; Hagan & McCarthy, 1997; McCarthy & Hagan, 1991), including property offenses (Baron, 2004; 2006; 2008; Baron & Hartnagel, 1997; McCarthy & Hagan, 1991), violent offenses (Baron & Hartnagel, 1998; Hagan & McCarthy, 1997; McCarthy & Hagan, 1991) and drug dealing (Baron, 1999; Baron & Hartnagel, 1997; McCarthy & Hagan, 1991). The likelihood that homelessness will lead to offending generally, and property offending in particular, is also greater when street youth have few moral barriers to breaking the law and/or when they have a low sense of self-efficacy or competence (Baron, 2004). In other words, youth who feel that they do not have the capacity to cope with their homelessness by legal means are more likely to resort to crime when they are homeless (Baron, 2004). Finally, "situational adversity" – situations of desperate need – can have a direct impact on offending. Research shows that hunger is directly associated with the theft of food and serious theft, while the need for shelter increases the likelihood of participation in more serious property crimes (Hagan & McCarthy, 1997).

Street Youth Unemployment and Crime

Most youth on the street are unemployed. Street youth are often unable to find work because of incomplete education and a lack of qualifications (Baron, 2001). These backgrounds exclude them from consideration for most jobs and from forms of employment that might offer opportunity for growth and advancement (Baron, 2001). Unemployment has been found to increase the probability that street youth will become involved in criminal activities (Baron, 2001; 2006; Baron & Hartnagel, 1997; Hagan & McCarthy, 1997). With no employment to be lost by criminal conduct, and work made irrelevant by its absence, street youth become more likely to

engage in crime. Unemployment can also reduce an individual's commitment to societal norms and rules, leading street youth to the conclusion that breaking the law is acceptable (Baron, 2008; Baron & Hartnagel, 1997). Unemployment may also contribute to feelings of boredom and frustration for some, who may view crime as one way to relieve these feelings (Baron, 2001; 2008; Baron & Hartnagel, 1997). Finally, unemployed youth are in need of money, which crime can provide. Beyond this direct impact, my research shows that unemployment is even more likely to lead to crime when youth have adopted values that support criminal activities (Baron, 2004).

Unemployment also produces a great deal of anger. Youth who want legitimate employment and are willing to work hard are understandably angry when they cannot find work. Homeless youth may feel they are unfairly deprived compared to others, blame others for their unemployment, be unhappy with their lack of money, and have peers involved in crime. This anger increases participation in violent offending and drug dealing (Baron, 2008; Baron & Hartnagel, 1997).

Street youth's experiences of frustration when trying to find work also leave them more likely to reject the idea that those who are willing to work hard will be able to achieve their economic goals. This disillusionment increases the likelihood that unemployment will lead to violent offending and drug distribution (Baron & Hartnagel, 1997). Further, perceiving their unemployment as unfair can lead to crime when youth have criminal peers and attitudes that support engaging in crime (Baron & Hartnagel, 2002).

Another key economic factor in street youth crime is relative deprivation. Relative deprivation occurs when people judge themselves to be worse off financially than other people or groups they know (Baron, 2004; 2006; 2008). My research reveals that relative deprivation increases participation in a range of offenses and is more likely to lead to crime when homelessness is long-term and the youth associates with criminally involved peers (Baron, 2006). Furthermore, being dissatisfied with their lack of money

compels street youth to engage in criminal activities particularly as the length of their homelessness and unemployment increases (Baron, 2004; 2006; 2008).

Finally, the goal of financial success also leads directly to general crime and drug dealing in the street youth population (Baron, 2006; McCarthy & Hagan, 2001). Wanting financial success and seeing no legal way to achieve it makes crime an attractive alternative (Baron, 2006). This is often the case when youth have experienced long-term homelessness and unemployment (Baron, 2006), and have values that encourage crime (Baron, 2011a).

Street Victimization and Crime

The experience of homelessness puts street youth at increased risk for victimization (Baron, 1997; Gaetz, 2004; Gaetz et al., 2010). Spending a great deal of time in high crime areas increases youth's vulnerability to property loss and damage, as well as risk of violent victimization (Baron, 1997; Gaetz, 2004; Gaetz et al., 2010). Further, homelessness may bring youth into contact with peers involved in crime who may victimize them (Baron, 1997; 2003a). Peers may steal from them, assault them, or encourage them to engage in conflicts where participants can end up as victims. Finally, the street subculture that encourages violence makes conflicts between youth more likely to turn violent (Baron, 1997; 2003a).

Many street youth are also regular users of drugs and alcohol, which increase their risk of victimization (Baron, 1997; 2003a; Baron & Hartnagel, 1997). First, these substances are often consumed in dangerous areas. Second, the biochemical and psychological impact of these substances can make youth less careful about their own safety, increasing the likelihood of theft or violent attack (Baron, 1997; 2003a). Users may also become more aggressive or provocative while using these substances, increasing the possibility of violent altercations (Baron, 1997; 2003a). At the same time, youth may be physically less able to defend themselves when intoxicated (Baron, 1997; 2003a).

Engaging in crime can also lead to victimization (Baron, 1997; 2003a; Gaetz, 2004). Illegal means of survival including drug dealing, robbery and theft have been found to be associated with violent victimization (Baron, 2003a). There is also a relationship between violent offending and victimization (Baron, 1997, 2003a; Baron, Forde, & Kennedy, 2007). Drug dealing or selling stolen property are high-risk activities, and street youth who engage in them become easy targets since they are unlikely to report their victimization to the police. Finally, violent offenders are continually at risk for retaliation from others who wish to settle scores (Baron & Hartnagel, 1998).

Experiences of victimization on the street often lead to criminal responses (Baron, 2009b; Baron & Hartnagel, 1998). First, people who experience victimization often feel unjustly harmed and learn from their victimization experiences that physical aggression may be necessary to ensure the safety of their property and themselves (Baron et al., 2001). Further, involvement in street peer groups, the public nature of the victimization, and subcultural expectations that encourage and reward retaliation against the offender, together increase the potential for retaliatory criminal responses in an effort to "get even" (Baron, 2009b; Baron, et al., 2001). I found that street youth who experience violent forms of victimization are more likely to engage in violent offences including 361 LEGAL & JUSTICE ISSUES group altercations (fights), minor and serious assaults, and robberies (Baron, 2004, 2009b; Baron & Hartnagel, 1998). Furthermore, being a victim of violence leads to violent crime when street youth also have values that support the use of violence and have high levels of self-efficacy and self-esteem. These characteristics appear to contribute to youth responding to their victimization with violence (Baron, 2004). Violent victimization is also more likely to lead to a violent response when youth have low self-control (Baron, 2009b). The experience of being robbed also provokes violent responses, and again those who have higher levels of self-esteem are able to draw on this resource to more successfully address their victimization. Property victimization

is also more likely to be met with violence when youth consider this a justified response (Baron, 2004).

Beyond direct victimization in terms of theft, robbery and physical attacks, the dangerous street environment also exposes street youth to "vicarious" victimization and the development of "anticipated" victimization (Baron, 2009b). Youth on the street frequently see or hear about others being victimized. Street youth come to expect that they will be victimized unless they take some form of defensive or pre-emptive action (Baron, 2009b). I found that (2009b) street youth exposed to vicarious victimization often undertook violent actions to prevent future harm to themselves and those around them, as well as for revenge against those deemed accountable for the harm. Exposure to the victimization of peers was more likely to evoke a violent response from street youth with low self-control. Similarly, expecting violent victimization was more likely to lead to a violent response from such youth (Baron, 2009b).

The Overall Experience of Coercion & the Link with Crime

My research shows that street youth's experience with formal state supervision through welfare or imprisonment can also lead to crime, in part because these systems are viewed as coercive. That is, people view them as negative experiences where they are forced or intimidated to act a certain way (Baron, 2009a; Colvin, 2000). State officials with the power to withdraw financial support (such as welfare), and inflict or threaten to impose punishment can coerce street youth (Baron, 2009a). There is evidence that youth who encounter more of these forms of coercion, along with other negative experiences, engage in more violent crime. I found (2009a) that the total combination of experiencing childhood abuse, street victimization, homelessness, receiving welfare, as well as imprisonment leads to a higher rate of violent offending. Further, youth who have this combination of experiences also tend to develop lower levels of self-control, higher levels of anger, greater

association with violent peers, and stronger values supportive of violence, when compared to those street youth who do not have these experiences. These factors, in turn, lead to higher levels of violence.

Drug and Alcohol Use and Crime

Another important contributor to street youth crime is drug and alcohol use. Studies suggest that offenders spend much of the money earned through criminal activity on drugs and alcohol (Baron, 1999; Baron & Hartnagel, 1997). Hartnagel and I (1997) found that drug and alcohol use were related to increased participation in property offending, and drug use was associated with drug dealing. While drug and alcohol use can be seen as a coping strategy to manage the negative emotions arising from traumatic backgrounds and difficult living situations in the present (Baron, 2004; 2010; Gallupe & Baron, 2009), these substances are also used as a form of enjoyment and recreation (Baron, 1999; Baron & Hartnagel, 1997). For some street youth, substance use provides an identity and social status among their peers (Baron, 1999; Baron & Hartnagel, 1997; 1998). Participation in crime as well as substance use may both be requirements for one to be accepted in the "street lifestyle" subculture, in order to take advantage of the social rewards it has to offer (Baron, 1999; Baron & Hartnagel, 1997; 1998). Over time, social contacts become increasingly limited to others involved in this lifestyle (Baron, 1999; Baron & Hartnagel, 1997; 1998). For participants, crime finances substance use, and substance use fuels the need for profitable crime to sustain an ever-increasing pattern of use (Baron, 1999; Baron & Hartnagel, 1997; 1998). Drug and alcohol use can also be important in facilitating criminal activities in another way. The use of these substances can make risky or difficult offenses psychologically easier to commit (Baron, 1999; Baron & Hartnagel, 1997; 1998). This type of influence may be important in understanding the link between drug and alcohol use and violent crime (Baron, 1997b; Baron & Hartnagel, 1998; Baron et al., 2007).

There is also some research to suggest that alcohol might be linked to lower violence (Baron et al., 2007). I argue along with Kennedy (1993) that there are subcultural rules on the street about substance use and violence. In some instances, street youth may be expected to ingest substances and act aggressively. In other settings, street youth may be encouraged to become intoxicated and socialize and relax with peers. In sum, different situations and settings may provide different rules regarding substance use and behaviours (Baron, 2003a; Baron e al., 2007; Kennedy & Baron, 1993).

[...]

References

Agnew, R. (2006). Pressured into crime: An overview of general strain theory. Los Angeles: Roxbury.

Anderson, E. (1999). Code of the street. New York: W.W. Norton.

Baron, S. W. (1995). Serious offenders. In J. Creechan & R. A. Silverman (Eds.), Canadian delinquency (pp.135-147). Toronto: Prentice-Hall.

Baron, S. W. (1997). Risky lifestyles and the link between offending and victimization. Studies on Crime and Crime Prevention, 6, 53-72.

Baron, S. W. (1999). Street youth and substance use: The role of background, subcultural, and economic factors. Youth & Society, 31(1), 3-26.

Baron, S. W. (2001). Street youth labour market experiences and crime. Canadian Review of Sociology and Anthropology, 38(2), 189-215.

Baron, S. W. (2003a). Street youth violence and victimization. Trauma, Violence, & Abuse, 4(1), 22-44.

Baron, S. W. (2003b). Self control, social consequences, and criminal behavior: Street youth and the general theory of crime. Journal of Research in Crime and Delinquency, 40(4), 403- 425.

Baron, S. W. (2004). General strain, street youth and crime: A test of Agnew's revised theory. Criminology, 42(2), 457-483.

Baron, S. W. (2006). Street youth, strain theory, and crime. Journal of Criminal Justice, 34(2), 209-223.

Baron, S. W. (2008). Street youth unemployment and crime: Is it that simple? Using general strain theory to untangle the relationship. Canadian Journal of Criminology and Criminal Justice,

50(4), 399-434.

Baron, S. W. (2009a). Differential coercion, street youth, and violent crime. Criminology, 47(1), 239-268.

Baron, S. W. (2009b). Street youths' violent responses to violent personal, vicarious, and anticipated strain. Journal of Criminal Justice, 37(5), 119-136.

Baron, S. W. (2010). Street youths' control imbalance and soft and hard drug use. Journal of Criminal Justice, 38(5), 903-912.

Baron S. W. (2011a). Street youths and the proximate and contingent causes of instrumental crime: Untangling anomie theory. Justice Quarterly, 28(3), 413-436.

Baron, S. W. (2011b). When formal sanctions encourage violent offending: How violent peers and violent codes undermine deterrence. Justice Quarterly. Advance online publication. doi:10. 1080/07418825.2011.633926

Baron, S. W., & Forde, D. R. (2007). Street youth crime: A test of control balance theory. Justice

Quarterly, 24(2), 335-355.

Baron, S. W., Forde, D. R., & Kay F. M. (2007). Self control, risky lifestyles, and situation. The role of opportunity and context in the general theory. Journal of Criminal Justice, 35(2), 119-136.

Baron, S. W., Forde, D. R. & Kennedy, L. W. (2007). Disputatiousness, aggressiveness, and victimization among street youths. Youth Violence and Juvenile Justice, 5(4), 411-425.

Baron S. W., & Hartnagel, T. F. (1997). Attributions, affect and crime: Street youths' reactions to unemployment. Criminology, 35(3), 409-434.

Baron, S. W., & Hartnagel, T. F. (1998). Street youth and criminal violence. Journal of Research in Crime and Delinquency, 35(2), 166-192.

Baron, S. W., & Hartnagel, T. F. (2002). Street youth and labor market strain. Journal of Criminal Justice, 30(6), 519-533.

Baron, S. W. & Kennedy, L. W. (1998). Deterrence and homeless male street youths. Canadian Journal of Criminology, 40(1), 27-60.

Baron, S. W., Kennedy, L. W., & Forde, D. R. (2001). Male street youths' conflict: The role of background, subcultural and situational factors. Justice Quarterly, 18(4), 759-789.

Baumeistser, R. F., Boden, J. M., & Smart, L. (1996). Relation of threatened egotism to violence and aggression: The dark side of high self-esteem. Psychological Review, 103(1), 5-33.

Chen, X., Thrane, L., Whitbeck, L. B., Johnson, K. D., & Hoyt, D. R. (2007). Onset of conduct disorder, use of delinquent subsistence strategies, and street victimization among homeless and runaway adolescents in the Midwest. Journal of Interpersonal Violence, 22(9), 1156-1183.

Colvin, M. (2000). Crime and coercion: An integrated theory of chronic criminality. NewYork: St. Martin's Press.

Forde, D. R., Baron, S. W., Scher, C., & Stein, M. B. (2012). Factor structure and reliability of the Childhood Trauma Questionnaire and prevalence estimates of trauma for male and female street-youth. Journal of Interpersonal Violence, 27(2), 364-379.

Forde, D. R., & Kennedy, L. W. (1997). Risky lifestyles, routine activities, and the general theory of crime. Justice Quarterly, 14(2), 265-294.

Gaetz, S. (2004). Safe streets for whom? Homeless youth, social exclusion and criminal victimization. Canadian Journal of Criminology and Criminal Justice, 46(4), 423-455.

Gaetz, S., & O'Grady, B. (2002). Making money: Exploring the economy of young homeless workers. Work, Employment and Society, 16(3), 433-456.

Gaetz, S., O'Grady, B., & Buccieri, K. (2010). Surviving crime and violence: Street youth and victimization in Toronto. Toronto: Justice for Children and Youth; Homeless Hub Press.

Gallupe, O., & Baron, S. W. (2009). Street youth, relational strain, and drug use. Journal of Drug Issues, 39(3), 523-546.

Gottfredson, M. R., & Hirschi, T. (1990). A general theory of crime. Stanford: Stanford University Press.

Hagan, J., & McCarthy, B. (1997). Mean streets: Youth crime and homelessness. Cambridge: Cambridge University Press.

Hay, C., & Forrest, W. (2006). The development of self-control: Examining self-control theory's stability thesis. Criminology, 44(4), 739-774.

Janus, M. D., Archambault, F. X., Brown, S. W., & Welsh, L. A. (1995). Physical abuse in Canadian runaway adolescents. Child Abuse & Neglect, 19(4), 433-447.

Kennedy, L. W., & Baron, S. W. (1993). Routine activities and a subculture of violence: A study of violence on the street. Journal of Research in Crime and Delinquency, 30(1), 88-113.

Kort-Butler, L. A., Tyler, K. A., & Melander, L. A. (2011). Childhood maltreatment, parental monitoring, and self-control among homeless young adults. Criminal Justice and Behavior, 38(12), 1244-1264.

McCarthy, B. (1996). The attitudes and actions of others: Tutelage and Sutherland's Theory of Differential Association. British Journal of Criminology, 36(1), 135-147.

McCarthy, B., & Hagan, J. (1991). Homelessness: A criminogenic situation? British Journal of Criminology, 31(4), 393-410.

McCarthy, B., & Hagan, J. (1992). Surviving on the street: The experiences of homeless youth. Journal of Adolescent Research, 7(4), 412-430.

McCarthy, B., & Hagan, J. (1995). Getting into street crime: The structure and process of criminal embeddedness. Social Science Research, 24(1), 63-95.

McCarthy, B. & Hagan, J. (2001). When crime pays: Capital, competence, and criminal success. Social Forces, 79(3), 1035-1060.

McCarthy, B., Hagan, J., & Cohen, L. W. (1998). Uncertainty, cooperation, and crime: Understanding the decision to co-offend. Social Forces, 77(1), 155-176.

O'Grady, B., Gaetz, S., & Buccieri, K. (2011). Can I see your ID? The policing of youth homelessness in Toronto. Toronto: Justice for Children and Youth; Homeless Hub.

Schreck, C. J., Wright, R. A., & Miller, J. M. (2002). A study of individual and situational antecedents of violent victimization. Justice Quarterly, 19(1), 159-180.

Stewart, E. A., & Simons, R. L. (2006). Structure and culture in African American adolescent violence: A partial test of the "Code of the Street" Thesis. Justice Quarterly, 23(1), 1-33.

Tanner, J., & Wortley, S. (2002). The Toronto youth leisure and victimization survey: Final report. Toronto: University of Toronto.

Tittle, C. R. (1995). Control balance: Toward a general theory of deviance. Boulder: Westview.

Tyler, K. A., & Johnson, K. A. (2006). A longitudinal study of the effects of early abuse on later victimization among high-risk adolescents. Violence and Victims, 21(4), 287-306.

Vaske, J., Ward, J. T., Boisvert, D., & Wright, J. P. (2012). The stability of risk-seeking from adolescence to emerging adulthood. Journal of Criminal Justice, 40(4), 313-322.

There Are Numerous Factors That Lead to Youth Being Homeless

National Network for Youth

The National Network for Youth (NN4Y) is a public organization who has spent the last 40 years putting efforts to helping youth avoid homelessness in America.

The Consequences Faced by Unaccompanied Youth & the Cost to Society

As a result of their homelessness, unaccompanied youth face devastating harms and barriers in life, all of which hinder their ability to re-assimilate into society, depress their motivation, and inhibit their becoming independent, successful, and contributing members of their families and communities. The consequences of homelessness bring despair to youth in the form of mental health problems, substance use, victimization and criminal activity, unsafe sexual practices, and barriers to education and employment. These problems further burden society with the cost of finding ways to take care of these youth. If these youth are not helped, they will likely become an addition to the population of chronic homeless adults.

Unaccompanied Youth Need Harm Reduced & Homes Found

Unaccompanied youth face a rough life when unstably housed, but they can be helped if their needs are addressed. Homelessness as an unaccompanied youth involves the horrors of survival sex, victimization, substance abuse, worsening mental health conditions, and barriers to education that turn into barriers to employment, and housing. Policymakers should put an end to the unjust consequences borne by homelessness by

"The Consequences of Youth Homelessness," National Network for Youth. Reprinted by permission.

investing in more affordable housing and supportive services for unaccompanied youth.

The Consequences of Youth Homelessness

1. Mental Health Problems

Unaccompanied youth are faced with the debilitating effects of mental health problems, caused by or made worse by homelessness. Half of all unaccompanied youth report mental health problems, which are predictors of chronic homelessness[1] . In studying these homeless youth, one finds that their mental health problems come in many forms. "Homeless adolescents often suffer from severe anxiety and depression...and low self-esteem. The rates of major depression, conduct disorder, and post-traumatic stress syndrome were found to be three times as high among runaway youth"[4] as among the general youth population. "Self-harming behaviors (cutting, burning, self-tattooing, etc.) are quite common"[5] among unaccompanied youth, as are suicide attempts. "Suicide is the leading cause of death among street youth."[5] Unfortunately, while mental health problems are prevalent among homeless youth, it is only a very small portion of these youth (a mere nine percent, at best) that have accessed mental health services.[3]

2. Substance Abuse

Many unaccompanied youth turn to substances to help deal with the stress and desperation caused by unstable living arrangements. Studies show that substance use among youth increases as living situations become "more stressful and less stable."[3] "Between 30 and 40 percent of unaccompanied youth report alcohol problems in their lifetime, and 40 to 50 percent report drug problems."[1] Unaccompanied youth are significantly more likely to use marijuana, crack cocaine, and other harmful substances than the general youth population.[3] Unfortunately, while the number of unaccompanied youth who turn to drugs and alcohol is high, the number of unaccompanied youth who find treatment is low (less than 15 percent).[3] Drug and alcohol abuse among unaccompanied

youth is dangerous, as it causes impairment, which leads to poor decision making.

3. *Criminal Activity & Victimization*

Homelessness leaves unaccompanied youth in a desperate situation, leading some to become involved in criminal activity. Many unaccompanied youth resort to illegal activity as part of their strategy for survival. For example, unaccompanied youth seeking shelter might break into an abandoned building, while youth seeking income to meet basic needs might prostitute themselves or sell drugs. One-fifth of unaccompanied youth report stealing. More than ten percent of homeless youth have forced entry into a residence. As many as half of homeless youth have participated in gang activity. [10] However, "while homeless youth often engage in criminal activity, research shows they are more likely to be the victims of crime rather than the perpetrators."[5] Trauma and rape rates among unaccompanied youth are two to three times higher than those of the general youth population. Unaccompanied youth often find themselves the victims of physical and sexual assault and robbery. [10] Regardless of their connections to crime, it is more effective to view delinquent unaccompanied youth as "young people in need of assistance, rather than as criminals."[2] Many times, youth are arrested by police officers who have no other ways to help. The criminal justice system is then used "as a means to assist youth [but] is generally counterproductive. Too often the youth is further stigmatized and exposed to additional criminal sophistication. The juvenile justice system is overwhelmed with violent and chronic offenders, and does not have the time or resources to devote to these [youth] or their needs."[2] Further, the costs of placing a homeless youth in the criminal justice system for one year ($53,665), a burden to be paid for by taxpayers, is significantly more than the cost ($5,887) of "permanently [moving] a homeless youth off the streets."[6] The poor decisions made by government and society regarding how to deal with unaccompanied youth (delinquent or

not) has resulted in a large and rather unnecessary loss of money and resources, with little to no benefit to the youth.

4. Unsafe Sexual Practices & Results

Many unaccompanied youth turn to prostitution for survival. This is known as survival sex, where sex is exchanged for money, shelter, food, or other necessities. The majority (95%) of homeless youth report being sexually active, with 13 years as the median age of first coitus. Over one-third of homeless youth report exchanging sex for food, shelter, or drugs.[7] Of the youth who engage in prostitution/ survival sex, the overwhelming majority trade sex for money. Approximately half also trade sex for temporary shelter, and one fifth trade sex for drugs. Most all homeless youth report that they engage in survival sex only when they are homeless.[10] Pregnancy rates among homeless youth are much higher than the rates of the general population, and seem to increase with the instability of a youth's housing situation. About 50% of street youth have had a pregnancy experience compared to about 33% living in shelters. Less than 10% of household youth have had a pregnancy experience.[14] "Homeless youth are three times as likely as national samples of youth to be pregnant, to have impregnated someone, or to already be a parent. Pregnancy may be the result of having no way to obtain money other than through prostitution (survival sex)."[1] To compound the problem, most homeless youth do not have access to information regarding sexual health and safety. "Homeless teen mothers showed a profound lack of knowledge or interest regarding birth control and reproductive health. 50% did not believe birth control was important."[12] With such high numbers of unaccompanied youth engaging in sex, it is dangerous to allow this population to continue to go without sexual health and safety education. Another result of this is the high rate of HIV and sexually transmitted illnesses in the homeless youth population. Because HIV prevention programs have been targeted at school-based youth, most unaccompanied youth are missed by these efforts.[7] Young people living on the street make up one of two

groups classified by the US Center for Disease Control as having the highest HIV prevalence in the United States.[5] Unaccompanied youth are significantly more likely to be diagnosed with HIV or die from AIDS as the general youth population. Studies find that, at any given moment, between 5 and 13 percent of unaccompanied youth are living with HIV. HIV prevalence for homeless youth may be as much as 2 to 10 times higher than the rates reported for other samples of adolescents in the United States.4

5. Barriers to Education & Employment

Unaccompanied youth face access barriers to education, keeping many of them from completing high school degrees or post-secondary education. Such barriers include school attendance policies, credit accrual, legal guardianship requirements,[9] residency requirements, proper records, and lack of transportation.[5] These barriers can cause youth to be denied enrollment, often resulting in a youth remaining out of school for long periods of time.[9] It is because of this that homelessness can interrupt education and normal socialization processes that are developed during youth. This affects a young person's future ability to live independently, [10] and also results in the development of learning problems and interpersonal communication problems, leading youth to have future troubles integrating into society. These problems, coupled with the lack of a degree, lead youth to face "severe challenges" in supporting themselves emotionally and financially." Without proper education or degree, unaccompanied youth find themselves contributing to unemployment rates in America. Those who can find jobs often don't make livable wages. Society will eventually feel the additional effects of uneducated and unemployed youth. "Youth who are out of school and out of work are not acquiring the knowledge and skills needed to replace the skilled, educated, and experienced adult workers who will be retiring in the coming decade."[11]

Further Statistics Concerning Consequences of Homelessness

Consequence: Mental Health Problems

- "Forty-five percent of homeless youth reported mental health problems in the past year."[1]
- 50 to 56 percent youth reported mental health problems over their lifetime."[1]
- "A mere 9 percent of [all] homeless youth [have] accessed mental health services."[3]
- Mental health problems are as much as eleven times higher for homeless youth than for the general population.[5]
- The rates of major depression, conduct disorder, and post-traumatic stress syndrome are 3 times as high among runaway youth as among the general population of youth.[4]
- 32% of homeless youth have attempted suicide. [2]

Consequence: Substance Abuse

- Homeless youth are 3 times more likely to use marijuana, and 18 times more likely to use crack cocaine than non-homeless youth.[3]
- Between 30 and 40 percent of homeless youth report alcohol problems in their lifetime, and 40 to 50 percent report drug problems.[1]
- Studies show that a mere 10 to 15 percent of all homeless youth are ever treated for drug and alcohol related problems.[3] !

Consequence: Criminal Activity

- 23 percent of homeless youth report stealing.[10]
- 14 percent of homeless youth have forced entry to a residence.[10]
- 20 percent of homeless youth report dealing drugs.[10]

- Runaway and homeless youth experience rape and assault rates 2 to 3 times higher than the general population of youth.[10]
- It costs $53,665 to maintain a youth in the criminal justice system for one year, but only $5,887 to permanently move a homeless youth off the streets.[6]

Consequence: Unsafe Sexual Practices

- 95 percent of homeless youth have engaged in sexual intercourse.[7]
- 13 years is the median age of first intercourse among homeless youth.[7]
- More than one third of homeless you engage in survival sex.[3]
- 75 percent of youth who engage in survival sex report only doing so while they are homeless.[10]
- Of the youth who engage in survival sex:
  - 82 percent trade sex for money. [10]
  - 48 percent trade sex for food or a place to stay. [10]
  - 22 percent trade sex for drugs.[10]
- Homeless youth are 7 times as likely to die from AIDS and 16 times as likely to be diagnosed with HIV as the general youth population.[3]
- About 50% of street youth have had a pregnancy experience compared to about 33% living in shelters. Less than 10% of household runaway youth have had a pregnancy experience.[14]
- A national study of homeless youth found the pregnancy rate of 13-15 year old homeless girls to be 14 percent, versus 1 percent for non-homeless girls. [13]
- 50 percent of homeless teen mothers did not believe birth control was important.[12]
- 41 percent of homeless teen mothers did not know they were pregnant until the second trimester. [12]
- HIV rates among homeless youth range from 5.3 percent to 12.9 percent.[4]

- HIV prevalence for homeless youth may be as much as 2 to 10 times higher than the rates reported for other samples of adolescents in the United States.[4]
- There are 162,000 homeless youth estimated to be victims of commercial sexual exploitation in the United States. [2]
- The average age of entry into prostitution is fourteen.[2]
- One of every three teens on the street will be lured into prostitution within 48 hours of leaving home. [2]

Youth Need Housing and Access to Specialized Programs & Treatment

1. Affordable Housing

Government and communities should offer more affordable housing to unaccompanied youth. Subsidized housing targeted to youth and young adults is imperative. Getting youth off the street and into a more stable housing situation will decreases the consequences associated with homelessness. Studies show that more stable housing situations decrease pregnancy rates and drug use among unaccompanied youth. Permanent housing will also takes youth away from streets where mental health deteriorates, give them permanent residency status which makes them eligible for public school enrollment, and will help prevent chronic homelessness. Housing would also prevent many unaccompanied youth from being victimized on the streets.

2. Programs and Treatment

Government and communities should offer more access to educational programs and treatment programs for homeless youth. Unaccompanied youth have need of assistance to help them deal with the consequences of homelessness. Youth would benefit from more substance abuse programs and treatment for mental health problems. In addition, unaccompanied youth would profit from safe sex education, and assistance in enrolling in other education programs. Easier access to basic needs (food, clothes,

etc.) would also decrease survival sex rates and crime rates among unaccompanied youth.

Sources

1. Burt, Martha R. (2007, June 19). Testimony. Subcommittee on Income Security and Family Support of the Ways and Means Committee of the US House of Representatives. Washington, DC.

2. Ekstrom, Bob. (n.d.). They can't work at McDonalds, so their choice is to sell drugs or themselves. Retrieved July 20, 2007 from http://www.windyouth.org/index.htm.

3. Ray, N. (2006). Lesbian, gay, bisexual and transgender youth: An epidemic of homelessness. New York: National Gay and Lesbian Task Force Policy Institute and the National Coalition for the Homeless.

4. National Coalition for the Homeless. (2006). NCH Fact Sheet #13: Homeless Youth. Retrieved July 20, 2007 from www.nationalhomeless.org/publications/facts/youth.pdf.

5. Common Ground. (n.d.). HYPE: Homeless Youth Peer Education Program. Retrieved July 26, 2007 from http:// www.commongroundwestside.org/homelessyouth.htm.

6. Unknown Author. (2007). Treatment for Homeless Youth Pays Off in Long Run. Retrieved July 19, 2007 from http:// www.huliq.com/7079/treatment-for-homeless-youth-pays-off-in-long-run.

7. Beech B.M., Myers L., Beech D.J., & Kernick N.S. (2003). Human immunodeficiency syndrome and hepatitis B and C infections among homeless adolescents. Seminars in Infectious Pediatric Diseases. Retrieved June 14, 2007, from PubMed database at http:// www.ncbi.nlm.nih.gov/sites/entrez.

8. Roy, Jessica. (April 10, 2007). New program works to keep teens off streets. Daily Bruin. Retrieved June 13, 2007 from http:// www.dailybruin.ucla.edu/news/2007/apr/10.

9. United States Department of Education. (2004). Education for homeless children and youth program. Retrieved July 9, 2007 from http://www.ed.gov/programs/homeless/guidance.pdf.

10. Robertson, M. J., & Toro, P. A. (1998). Homeless Youth: Research, Intervention, and Policy. Retrieved June 18, 2007 from http://aspe.hhs.gov/homeless/symposium/3-Youth.htm.

11. Mincy, Ronald B. (2007, June 19). Testimony. Subcommittee on Income Security and Family Support of the Ways and Means Committee of the US House of Representatives. Washington, DC.

12. Homes for the Homeless. (2003). Teen Pregnancy Report. Retrieved June 26, 2007 from http:// www.homesforthehomeless.com/index.asp?CID=1&PID=36&NID =52.

13. American Civil Liberties Union. (2003). Letter to the House Urging Opposition to the Musgrave Amendment to HR 1925, the Runaway, Homeless, and Missing Children Protection Act. Retrieved June 7, 2007 from http://www.aclu.org/reproductiverights/contraception/12528leg20030514.html.

14. Greene, J.M., & Ringwalt, C.L. (1998). Pregnancy among three national samples of runaway and homeless youth. Journal of Adolescent Health, Volume 23, Issue 6. Retrieved June 7, 2007 from http://www.jahonline.org/article/PIIS1054139X98000718/ abstract.

Parental Abuse and Violence Lead to Future Crime and Homelessness for Youth

John Hagan and Bill McCarthy

John Hagan and Bill McCarthy are professors in the Department of Sociology at the University of California, Davis, who share research interests of incarceration and crime.

Abstract

This paper tests the thesis that childhood experiences of parental abuse and violence, and the resulting shame spirals these produce, may be predisposing life experiences mac interact with later criminal justice sanctions to intensify involvements in crime and diversion from contacts and experiences that lead to legal work. Yet not all street youth have these destructive experiences or react to their environments in this way, with resilience being in this sense the alternative reaction of a significant number of street youth co their crime on the street. Our data on street youth confirm that family backgrounds of crime and abuse interact with the experience of homeless youth being charged by the police and becoming further involved in theft behavior, while alternatively it is the minority of homeless youth who escape police contact and the shaming process it intensifies who are more likely to associate with legally employed peers. We argue that it is most often the latter less scathed street youth who can move along an important avenue of escape that can lead to legal employment and away from the street.

Introduction

Risk and resilience are salient themes in the transitions to adulthood of homeless youth. Perhaps the most prevalent risk for homeless youth in the period of emerging adulthood is the

"The Shame in Their Game: Homelessness, Youth Crime, and Transitions Toward Work," by John Hagan and Bill McCarthy, UC Davis Department of Sociology. Reprinted by permission.

prospect of escalating contact with the juvenile and criminal justice systems. Homeless youth not only may be involved in crime, but they also by definition lack access to private space and therefore disproportionately occupy the public space of the street, where they are at elevated risk of contact with the police. These en counters can have a self-fulfilling quality, with police contacts not only bringing potential punishment, but as well perpetuating stigmatized feelings of shame and embarrassment that amplify identification and involvement which street subcultures of crime.

The result is that homeless youth tend to travel the streets that they occupy in one way--in the direction leading away from adults and peers who can assist them in forming links into employment opportunities that facilitate escape from homeless. Still, not all homeless youth are caught up in the criminal justice system, and the implication is that some homeless youth can reverse the course of their lives by pursuing employment opportunities that lead away from adult criminals and peers and their high risk lives on the street. The challenge is to capture the realities of both risk and resilience on the meet and their relationship co one another. For policy purposes, the challenge is co distinguish those youth who are caught in the life of the meet from those who are not, so as to increase our understanding and ideally our leverage over those factors that may be amenable to changes and that can improve the odds of successful transitions to adulthood among homeless youth. The thesis of this paper is that limited contact with the justice system is a crucial factor, especially for emotionally vulnerable youth, in preserving the prospects for successfully leaving the street for the more conventional world of legal work.

Studying the Street

UNICEF (1989) estimates that approximately 100 million children and adolescents live on the streets of cities worldwide. Although conditions obviously vary, homeless youth represent an important and sizable proportion of the adolescents living in high-risk settings of both developed (Wright 1991) and developing nations of the

world [National Research Council 1993: 182; UNICEF 1998; see also Apcekar 1988; Wright, Wittig and Kaminsky 1993; Campos, Raffaelli and Ude 1994). Although an estimated two-fifths of the world's street youth live in Latin America (Barker and Knaul 1991), with a majority of these youth living on the meets of Brazil (Campos et al. 1994), homeless youth sleep on the streets in Europe (Avramov 1998); Russia (Stephenson 2001; Stoecker 2001); India (Ganesan 1996); the rest of Asia, Africa (Swarr 1990) and Australia (Downing-Orr 1996)]. In the United States, 1999 estimates from the Department of Health and Human Services i ndicate that the meet youth population ranged from one-half to one and a third million (also see Shane 1989).

The risk and resilience themes that characterize the lives of homeless youth place them at the focal point of a recent critique by Loic Wacquant (2002) of urban street ethnography. The most notable target of Wacquant's critique is, for our purposes, Katherine Newman's (1999) book, *No Shame in My Game: The Working Poor in the Inner City*. While Newman's study does not focus on homeless youth per se, it ad dresses an issue that we have already noted is apparent among these young people, namely, that againsc all odds, some socially and economically disadvantaged street youth find and pursue legal employment.

Newman emphasizes in her research that paid legal work is an important pare of life in even the most impoverished African-American communities. This attention to the working poor is intentionally contrasted in Newman' s work with the focus on the job less underclass that is central w the writing of Wacquanr and his mentor, William Julius Wilson (e.g., Wacquant and Wilson 1993). Newman argues that Wacquant is too preoccupied with what we have identified as the first theme above--the risks that link poverty to crime and arrest -- to properly appreciate a second theme that characterizes life in the inner city, the resilience of the working poor. As Newman (2002: 1578-1579) explains,

"Ethnographic work on the inner city has fixated on deviance behavior. However, a central contention of my book is that life

in the African-American inner city is not predominately focused on Wacquant's under-class end of the street. Sociologists have so emphasized the presence of gangs, drugs, and hustlers that they have forgotten that paid work has been and remains a central and de fining activity for many African-American residents of the ghetto. Even in the most impoverished neighborhoods in the Urban Family Life Survey at the University of Chicago to which Wacquant contributed, more than one-third of die respondents in the poorest neighborhoods were working and over half were either in the labor force or in school ... Where are the ghetto workers in the research and theory that emerged from the underclass tradition? They are barely mentioned."

The same point can and should be made about homeless and working street youth, because there are homeless youth who successfully find legal work and escape all contact with the justice system, and their success needs co be noted and explained.

Wacquant's (2002: 1512) response co Newman is that she is too sanguine about the choices and possibilities that western, post-industrial labor markets present poor and minority youth with. Wacquant sees a myopic optimism in Newman' s view of contemporary class circumstances:

... "in language evocative of l 9'h century ideologues of ascending industrial capitalism (and contemporary neoconservatives), Newman presents most ghetto youths as 'free to choose' between drug dealing and legitimate employment, between welfare check and paycheck, and between the shame of state 'dependency' and the honor of servile wage work ... Counting these alternative paths in (and out of) the local socio-economic structure in terms of individual volition and discretion thwarts *the analysis of the mechanisms and condition under which differently positioned youth follow this or that circuit and with what consequences"* (emphasis added).

This critique is both methodological and theoretical, with Wacquant arguing (2002: 1504) that by focusing in her study largely on youth who are employed, Newman effectively samples on the dependent variable and thereby occludes the source of variation

in employment outcomes that is necessary to rest the mechanisms and conditions that lead away from the street and joblessness.

Newman actually does give attention to youth who do not get jobs and she is fully aware of the constraints as well as the choices that destitute youth confront. What more dearly distinguishes Newman from Wacquant is her focus on resilience in the lives of the young, working poor, and the possibility that these young people at lease sometimes can find routes that lead away from the alternative risks of urban street life. Newman (2002: 1579) insists that these youth are a crucial part of the story of the streets.

[…]

Untreated Mental Illness Is Connected to Homelessness and Criminal Activity

Best MSW Programs

Best MSW Programs is an online resource for locating the top Master's in Social Work degree programs, offering reviews, rankings, and scholarship information for MSW students.

About a fifth of America's 1.7 million homeless population suffer from untreated schizophrenia or manic depressive illness. That translates, if you can imagine it, to 385,000 individuals, roughly more than the population of cities such as Dayton, Des Moines, Ft. Lauderdale, Grand Rapids, Providence, Richmond, or Salt Lake City. And of that number, a percentage will wind up in prison.

The facts about homelessness get even worse when you break down the numbers. According to the National Coalition for the Homeless, when you focus in on single adult homeless males, about 16 percent of them suffer from some form of severe and persistent mental illness.

Not surprisingly, mental illness often prolongs homelessness. Approximately 26 percent of homeless adults staying in shelters live with serious mental illness and an estimated 66 percent live with severe mental illness and/or substance use disorders.

At any given moment in time, there are many more people with untreated severe psychiatric illnesses living on America's streets than are receiving care in America's hospitals. To wit: approximately 90,000 individuals with schizophrenia or manic-depressive illness are in all hospitals receiving treatment for their disease.

Despite the disproportionate number of severely mentally ill people among the homeless population, most experts on the subject

"Madness in the Streets: Mental Illness, Homelessness and Criminal Behavior," Best MSW Programs, 2017. Reprinted by permission.

The Problem of Homelessness in the U.S.

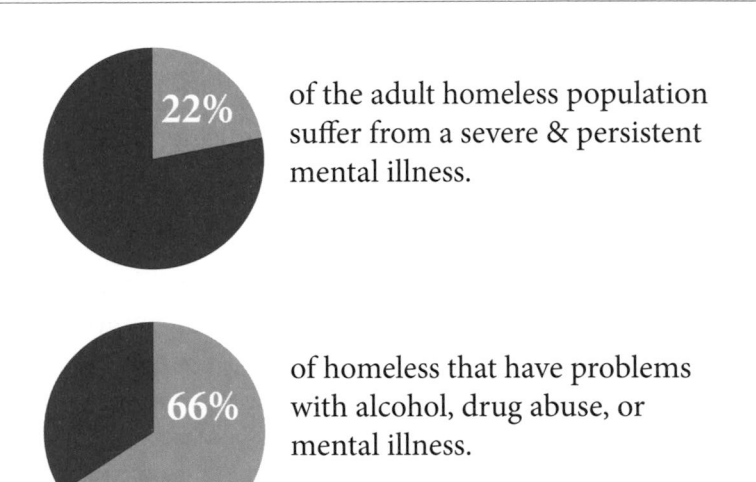

1,750,000 Number of homeless people in the U.S.

Number of people who experience
homelessness on any given night in the U.S. 610,042

22% of the adult homeless population suffer from a severe & persistent mental illness.

66% of homeless that have problems with alcohol, drug abuse, or mental illness.

SOURCE: National Coalition for the Homeless

do not believe that increases in homelessness are attributable to the release of severely mentally ill people from institutions.

Indeed, most patients were released from mental hospitals in the 1950s and 1960s, yet vast increases in homelessness did not occur until the 1980s, when incomes and housing options for those living on the margins began to diminish rapidly. Most homeless persons with mental illness do not need to be institutionalized, but can live in the community with the appropriate supportive

housing options. Problem is, many mentally ill homeless people cannot obtain access to supportive housing and/or other treatment services. And state and city budgets have been drastically cut, leaving the mentally ill, and other less fortunate, literally out in the streets. Some of those people turn to crime.

Mental Illness and Crime

Although prevalence rates vary considerably across studies, there is general agreement among researchers that the number of mentally ill individuals in jail is substantial, and that many of these individuals are arrested for minor crimes, particularly disorderly conduct. There is evidence that a large percentage of jailed individuals may also have been homeless at the time of arrest. The most striking finding was that nearly 21% were classified

Formerly Homeless Now in Prison

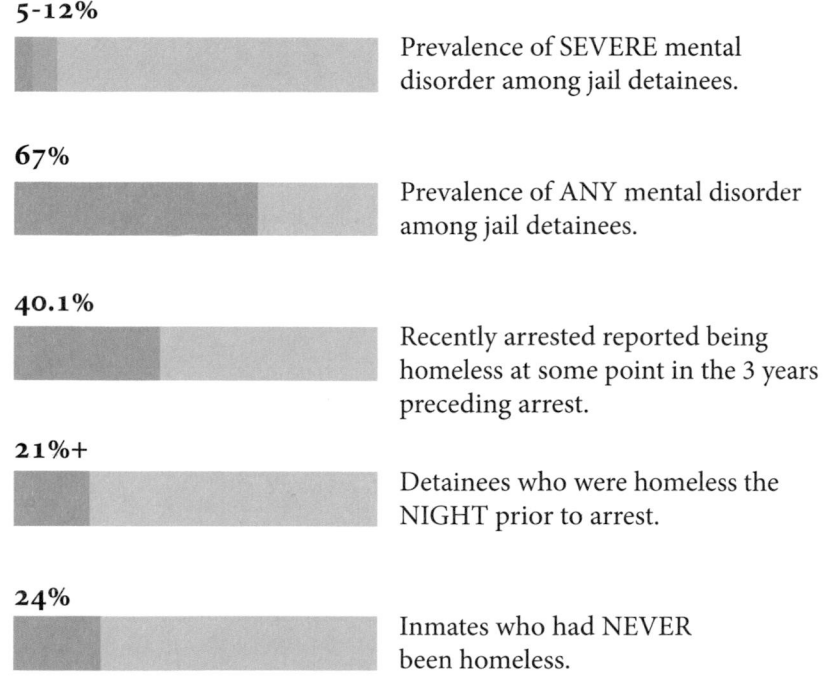

5-12%

Prevalence of SEVERE mental disorder among jail detainees.

67%

Prevalence of ANY mental disorder among jail detainees.

40.1%

Recently arrested reported being homeless at some point in the 3 years preceding arrest.

21%+

Detainees who were homeless the NIGHT prior to arrest.

24%

Inmates who had NEVER been homeless.

SOURCE: National Coalition for the Homeless

as homeless when they were arrested and 40 percent said they had been homeless at some time during the past few years. The researchers concluded that homelessness significantly increases the risk of indictment for violent criminal offenses among mentally disordered offenders (MDOs).

Problems associated with being homeless are compounded when homeless individuals also have a history of hospitalization for a mental disorder. Homeless persons with a history of prior hospitalization in a mental health facility also had greater involvement in criminal activities than homeless individuals with no such history. In New York City, researchers looked into what type of crimes are committed by the homeless.

Homelessness and Crime

Once incarcerated, even stronger links between mental illness, homelessness and crime were found. Prison inmates who had been homeless (that is, those who reported an episode of homelessness anytime in the year before incarceration) made up 15.3 percent of the U.S. jail population, or 7.5 to 11.3 times the standardized estimate of 1.36 -to 2.03 percent in the general U.S. adult population. Compared to other inmates, those who were homeless were more likely to be currently incarcerated for a property crime, but they were also more likely to have past criminal justice system involvement for both nonviolent and violent offenses, to have mental health and substance abuse problems, to be less educated, and to be unemployed.

Homelessness and incarceration appear to increase the risk of each other, and these factors seem to be mediated by mental illness and substance abuse, as well as by disadvantageous socio-demographic characteristics. Criminal behavior appears to serve various functions among the homeless, and the homeless who engaged in illegal behavior can be classified as chronic criminals, supplemental criminals, criminals out of necessity, substance abusers, or the mentally ill. While the homeless as a whole engage in

relatively high levels of illegal activity, for many, this is an adaptive response to dealing with severely limited resources.

Health Insurance and The Affordable Care Act

The links between homelessness, mental illness and crime could possibly be broken by the Affordable Care Act. For many of the homeless, it's the very lack of access to health insurance that leads to a constant struggle to survive. By not having health insurance, people who are homeless often forgo treatment for mental illness, substance use, chronic health conditions, acute care and injuries making it difficult to focus on the goal of finding housing.

Without health insurance, mental health and medical crises and ongoing related costs can lead a lower-income household down the path to homelessness and in some cases, criminal behavior. The Affordable Care Act could help in providing a safety net of needed services, insurance coverage plays a critical role in helping a person who is homeless access those services needed to regain stability – mental, physical, and residential. Linking people who are homeless to Medicaid – the health insurance program for lower – income Americans – has become an increasingly important federal priority, and might, in the long term, help decrease the number of criminal acts performed by homeless individuals.

More Needs to Be Done to Help the Homeless

Bill Quigley

A hurricane Katrina survivor, Bill Quigley is the Associate Director of the Center for Constitutional Rights as well as a law professor at Loyola University in New Orleans.

Three True Stories

Renee Delisle was one of over 3500 homeless people in Santa Cruz when she found out she was pregnant. The Santa Cruz Sentinel reported she was turned away from a shelter because they did not have space for her. While other homeless people slept in cars or under culverts, Renee ended up living in an abandoned elevator shaft until her water broke.

Jerome Murdough, 56, a homeless former Marine, was arrested for trespass in New York because he was found sleeping in a public housing stairwell on a cold night. *The New York Times* reported that one week later, Jerome died of hypothermia in a jail cell heated to over 100 degrees.

Paula Corb and her two daughters lost their home and have lived in their minivan for four years. They did laundry in a church annex, went to the bathroom at gas stations, and did their studies under street lamps, according to America Tonight.

Fact One. Over half a million people are homeless

On any given night, there are over 600,000 homeless people in the US according to the US Department of Housing and Urban Development (HUD). Most people are either spending the night in homeless shelters or in some sort of short term transitional housing. Slightly more than a third are living in cars, under bridges or in some other way living unsheltered.

"Ten Facts about Being Homeless in USA", by Bill Quigley, Common Dreams, October 14, 2014. http://www.commondreams.org/views/2014/10/14/ten-facts-about-being-homeless-usa. Licensed under CC BY SA 3.0.

Fact Two. One quarter of homeless people are children

HUD reports that on any given night over 138,000 of the homeless in the US are children under the age of 18. Thousands of these homeless children are unaccompanied according to HUD. Another federal program, No Child Left Behind, defines homeless children more broadly and includes not just those living in shelters or transitional housing but also those who are sharing the housing of other persons due to economic hardship, living in cars, parks, bus or train stations, or awaiting foster care placement. Under this definition, the National Center for Homeless Education reported in September 2014 that local school districts reported there are over one million homeless children in public schools.

Fact Three. Tens of thousands of veterans are homeless

Over 57,000 veterans are homeless each night. Sixty percent of them were in shelters, the rest unsheltered. Nearly 5000 are female.

Fact Four. Domestic violence is a leading cause of homelessness in women

More than 90% of homeless women are victims of severe physical or sexual abuse and escaping that abuse is a leading cause of their homelessness.

Fact Five. Many people are homeless because they cannot afford rent

The lack of affordable housing is a primary cause of homelessness according to the National Law Center on Homelessness and Poverty. HUD has seen its budget slashed by over 50% in recent decades resulting in the loss of 10,000 units of subsidized low income housing each and every year.

Fact Six. There are fewer places for poor people to rent than before

One eighth of the nation's supply of low income housing has been permanently lost since 2001. The US needs at least 7 million more affordable apartments for low income families and as a result millions of families spend more than half their monthly income on rent.

Fact Seven. In the last few years millions have lost their homes

Over five million homes have been foreclosed on since 2008, one out of every ten homes with a mortgage. This has caused even more people to search for affordable rental property.

Fact Eight. The Government does not help as much as you think

There is enough public rental assistance to help about one out of every four extremely low income households. Those who do not receive help are on multi-year waiting lists. For example, Charlotte just opened up their applications for public housing assistance for the first time in 14 years and over 10,000 people applied.

Fact Nine. One in five homeless people suffer from untreated severe mental illness

While about 6% of the general population suffers from severe mental illness, 20 to 25% of the homeless suffer from severe mental illness according to government studies. Half of this population self-medicate and are at further risk of addiction and poor physical health. A University of Pennsylvania study tracking nearly 5000 homeless people for two years discovered that investing in comprehensive health support and treatment of physical and mental illnesses is less costly than incarceration, shelter and hospital services for the untreated homeless.

Fact Ten. Cities are increasingly making homelessness a crime

A 2014 survey of 187 cities by the National Law Center on Homelessness & Poverty found: 24% make it a city-wide crime to beg in public; 33% make it illegal to stand around or loiter anyplace in the city; 18% make it a crime to sleep anywhere in public; 43% make it illegal to sleep in your car; and 53% make it illegal to sit or lay down in particular public places. And the number of cities criminalizing homelessness is steadily increasing.

The Homeless Have Many Crimes Committed Against Them

National Coalition for the Homeless

The NCH is a national organization in the U.S. with one single mission: to prevent and put an end to homelessness while assuring that the rights of the homeless are protected.

Executive Summary

The National Coalition for the Homeless (NCH) has documented 1,650 acts of violence against homeless individuals by housed perpetrators over the past 17 years (1999-2015). These crimes are believed to have been motivated by the perpetrators' biases against people experiencing homelessness or by their ability to target homeless people with relative ease. The crimes include an array of atrocities such as murder, beatings, rapes, and even mutilations.

NCH has found startling data regarding the number and severity of attacks. However, the true calamity may be even worse that these reports imply. Because the homeless community is treated so poorly in our society, many attacks go unreported and unrepresented. Therefore, we cannot know the full scope of these abuses. Hate crimes against the homeless community are a vital issue in need of public attention.

Over the last 17 years, NCH has determined the following:

- 1,657 reported acts of violence have been committed against individuals experiencing homelessness
- 428 victims have lost their lives as a result of the attacks
- Reported violence has occurred in 48 states, Puerto Rico, and the District of Columbia
- Perpetrators of these attacks were generally males under age 30; most commonly they were teenage boys.

"No safe Street: A Survey Of Hate Crimes and Voilence Committed Against Homeless People in 2014-2015," National Coalition for the Homeless, July, 2016. Reprinted by permission.

Specifically, in 2014:

- There were 122 victims of attacks against people experiencing homelessness.
- 26 of the victims of these attacks lost their lives.
- 82% of all perpetrators whose ages are reported were under the age of 30
- 95% of all perpetrators whose genders are reported were male
- 74% of victims whose ages are reported were over the age of 40
- 81% of all victims whose genders are reported were male
  Specifically, in 2015:
- There were 77 victims of attacks against people experiencing homelessness
- 27 of the victims of these attacks lost their lives.
- 73% of perpetrators whose ages are reported were under the age of 30
- 90% of all perpetrators whose genders are reported were male
- 57% of victims whose ages are reported were over the age of 40
- 77% of all victims whose genders are reported were male

No Safe Street: A Survey of Hate Crimes and Violence Committed against Homeless People in 2014 & 2015 documents the known cases of violence against individuals experiencing homelessness by housed individuals in those two years. The report includes descriptions of the cases, current and pending legislation that would help protect homeless people, and recommendations for advocates to help prevent violence against homeless individuals.

Purpose

The main objective of this report is to educate lawmakers, advocates, and the general public about hate crimes and violence against the homeless community, in order to bring about change and ensure the protection of civil rights for everyone, regardless of economic circumstances or housing status. As part of its mission,

NCH is committed to creating the systemic and attitudinal changes necessary to end homelessness. A large component of these changes must include the societal guarantee of safety and protection, as well as a commitment by lawmakers to combat hate crimes and other violent acts against people who experience homelessness.

Methodology

The data on violent acts committed against the homeless population were gathered from a variety of sources including published national and local news reports. Homeless advocates and local service providers across the country also provided information about incidents in their local communities. In addition, this report relied on the voices of homeless persons and formerly homeless people, who self-reported incidents they experienced firsthand.

Every reported incident was subject to a rigorous fact-checking process, designed to evaluate and verify the accuracy of the reported events. This process entailed multiple follow-up discussions with those closely involved with the incident. Cross-comparisons were also made with other news sources reporting the incident.

While the motive for each attack was not always evident from the information available, in many cases, there was confirmation that these violent acts were perpetrated because of a bias against the victim based on her or his housing status. Other acts were deemed opportunistic and committed merely because the homeless person, due to the nature of homelessness, was in a vulnerable position that turned her or him into an easy target. Only attacks perpetrated by housed individuals against un-housed individuals were evaluated. Crimes committed by homeless people against other homeless persons were excluded from this report.

Although NCH has made every effort to verify the facts regarding each incident included in this report, new information about cases may become available after its publication. For this reason, the NCH constantly researches and reviews all facts related to the included data. As additional evidence emerges about prior,

new, or previously unknown cases, it is the policy of NCH to adjust tabulations based on the new information.

Now and Then: Hate Crimes Against the Homeless, 1999-2015

A hate crime is defined by the U.S. Department of Justice's Federal Bureau of Investigation (FBI) as a "criminal offense committed against a person, property, or society that is motivated, in whole or part, by the offender's bias."

The FBI does not currently recognize protected status for people experiencing homelessness.[1] Over the past 17 years, NCH has recorded 1,650 incidents of crimes committed against this unprotected group. In 2014 and 2015, NCH became aware of 192 attacks, 58 of which resulted in death. While these statistics are alarming on their own, it is also important to note that people experiencing homelessness are often treated so poorly by society that attacks are forgotten or unreported. It is possible that the number of attacks was much higher.

Without shelter, the homeless population is particularly vulnerable to both the elements of nature and the abuses of society. Once homeless, their suffering can be a vicious cycle of frustrating attempts to regain housing. Many communities do not have shelter space or adequate affordable housing to meet their needs. According to the U.S. Department of Housing and Urban Development, on a single night in 2014 there were 578,424 homeless people in the United States, including 362,163 who were homeless as individuals and 216,261 who were homeless in families.[2]

Violence against the homeless by housed individuals is an alarming trend that has increased steadily from year to year since 1999 when NCH began recording incidents. In 2014 alone, there were 11 more fatal attacks (29) compared to 2013 (18), a 61% increase. There was also a 17% increase in nonlethal attacks over the same period. In 2015, 29 fatal attacks were recorded, the same as in the previous year. It is important to note, however, that the

total number of attacks recorded was lower (115 attacks in 2014, 77 attacks in 2015).

[…]

Endnotes

1 U.S. Department of Justice Federal Bureau of Investigation. Hate Crime http://www.fbi.gov/about- us/investigate/civilrights/hate_crimes/overview
2 Office of Planning and Development, U.S. Department of Housing and Urban Development. The 2013 Part 1 Point-in-Time Estimates of Homelessness. November 2013

CHAPTER 2

Are the Homeless More Likely to Be Found Guilty of a Crime?

Overview: There Is a Direct Correlation Between Homelessness and Crime

Stephen Metraux, Caterina G. Roman, and Richard S. Cho

Stephen Metraux is the Deputy Director of Research for the National Center for Homelessness Among Veterans as well as an Associate Professor of Health Policy and Public Health at the University of the Sciences in Philadelphia. Caterina G. Roman is on the faculty of Temple University's Department of Criminal Justice. Richard S. Cho served as Deputy Director of U.S. Interagency Council on Homelessness.

Introduction

Over the past 25 years the United States has seen large increases in both incarceration and homelessness. The jail and prison population went from approximately 500,000 in 1980 to 2.1 million in 2004 (Pastore & MacGuire, 2005), while the homeless population transformed from a small collection of individuals stereotyped as bums and winos to a diverse assortment of families and individuals that, according to best estimates, now include at least 2.3 million who are homeless at some point in a year (Burt et al., 1999). Little is known, however, about the relationship between these two concurrent phenomena. Although service providers have long pointed to anecdotal evidence about the overlap between these two populations, awareness of this nexus from a research perspective is relatively recent and in its nascent stages.

This paper presents evidence for evaluating two assumptions. The first assumption is that persons who are homeless are at increased risk for incarceration and, conversely, release from jail or prison leaves a person particularly vulnerable to an episode of homelessness. Much of the research on the homelessness-incarceration nexus is still documenting parameters. Specifically,

"Incarceration and Homelessness," by Stephen Metraux, Caterina G. Roman and Richard S. Cho, U.S. Department of Housing and Urban Development.

this includes the rates at which people cross over from one to the other; the proximate factors associated with an increased probability of such crossovers; and more general explanations of why such a high degree of crossover exists.

The second assumption concerns the centrality of housing, coupled with supports (in whatever form they may take) that help to maintain this housing, in preventing both homelessness and incarceration among persons at risk for both. For those who lack the resources and supports to obtain secure housing upon release, providing such housing stands to mitigate the risks for both homelessness and reincarceration.

Evaluating this assumption involves examining the more general experience faced by persons who reenter the community from jails and prisons, as well as examining empirical evidence on outcomes related to interventions that involve housing and supports. Service and housing providers have given limited attention and resources to addressing the needs presented by persons with histories of both incarceration and homelessness. When they have done so, the tendency has been to adapt other models rather than to develop specific interventions focusing on the specific problems presented by this population. Interventions that do exist, whether adapted from other housing models or designed specifically to address the needs of this population, typically are ahead of the research literature on best practices. This paper will review the range of housing approaches, featuring specific housing programs within this continuum, and what, in the absence of extensive evidence in this field, is considered to be best practice.

In describing what will be covered, it is also necessary to outline the limits as to what will be covered here. Community reentry (for persons released from incarceration) and homelessness are both broad topics that touch on a range of other topics. Focusing on the immediate nexus of these two topics necessarily steals attention from areas with a less direct bearing. For example, responses toward this problem do not, by and large, address more general policies regarding incarceration and housing, although this will ultimately

be the solution to this problem. Similarly, more general topics such as employment, healthcare, education, and stigma figure into understanding this nexus, but are only touched on in this paper. And some related topics, such as how incarceration of an adult may lead to collateral homelessness for family members, are important but lack research and interventions that provide clearer understanding. This need for future research is addressed in the final section. Opportunities here abound, as knowledge of the nature of the problem and evidence to support current intervention practices still contain numerous gaps with respect to many key questions.

Policy and Institutional Context

This link between incarceration and homelessness can be viewed as a second wave of deinstitutionalization. Deinstitutionalization is a term traditionally used in reference to the exodus of persons treated for mental illness from psychiatric hospitals to the community (i.e., the "first wave"), and it has parallels to the more recent interactions between carceral institutions and homelessness. The problematic implementation of deinstitutionalization left many persons with mental illness to enter the community unprepared and unsupported, and has been widely thought to be the reason why, from the 1980s on, persons with mental illness figured prominently among the rolls of the homeless population. By comparison, rates of shelter use have been found to be higher among people exiting prison than among people exiting state psychiatric hospitals (Metraux & Culhane, 2004). The number of people exiting prisons and jails to the community was 650,000 and 9 million, respectively, in 2004 alone (Brown, 2006; Harrison & Beck, 2006); just the number of those released from prison alone dwarfs the number deinstitutionalized from psychiatric hospitals (Mechanic & Rochefort, 1990).

Actors involved in this current round of deinstitutionalization involving the criminal justice system can learn from some of the missteps of the previous round of deinstitutionalization

involving the mental health system. One key lesson from deinstitutionalization of persons from psychiatric hospitals has been the importance of housing. For the deinstitutionalized mentally ill population, housing had been viewed by community mental health services as a public welfare function, and was largely ignored until homelessness became linked with mental illness. Only as a result of this link did there emerge a consensus in the community mental health field that housing is, in fact, a mental health service and a prerequisite to effectively providing other forms of community-based services (Metraux, 2002). This is an example of where the criminal justice system appears to have learned little from the mistakes made in deinstitutionalizing persons who are mentally ill. The lack of jurisdictional clarity over the problem of post-incarceration homelessness means that people who are homeless at the point of their discharge from incarceration fall under the purview of neither the corrections system, which views its jurisdiction over inmates as ending at discharge, nor the homeless assistance system, as individuals leaving institutions are not considered presently homeless and are therefore ineligible for most forms of homeless assistance. Cho (2004) attributes this jurisdictional gap to a condition of "isolationist policymaking," in which sectors of government define their spheres of responsibility too narrowly thus leaving some individuals to become "institutional refugees." As Black and Cho (2004) explain, the result is ultimately a scarcity of public funding and resources that target persons who are homeless upon their release from incarceration. As a result, people leaving incarceration enter an uncertain transitional space between institution and community in which services are fragmented at the point where they are most vulnerable (Hopper & Baumohl, 1994).

What Has Changed Since 1998?

Criminal justice involvement among people who are homeless is hardly new: jails and detention facilities have historically served as de facto institutions for persons who were homeless when they were picked up either for violating vagrancy laws or as a benevolent

means of quartering (Hopper, 2003). Likewise, shelter operators and other homeless housing providers have long reported seeing high rates of people with recent experiences in correctional settings among their clientele. Some providers of homeless shelters have anecdotally reported rates of formerly incarcerated people as high as 70 percent (Cho, 2004), while a national survey of providers of homeless services conducted in 1996 found that " ltogether, 54 percent [of persons receiving homeless services] have some experience of incarceration" (Burt et al., 1999).

What is new is a growing level of concern. In terms of reentry, this concern has manifested itself in a changing political climate in which there is a greater receptiveness towards attending to problems related to reentry (Suellentrop, 2006). A recent analysis by Jacobson (2005) suggests that developments in the current political climate may further facilitate efforts to increase programming to address the needs of the formerly incarcerated. In this argument, the huge swell in the prison population, negative public opinions about crime and public safety, and interest in curbing or rethinking public spending practices all create a window of opportunity for policymakers and leaders to create and implement programs that hold the promise of slowing incarceration rates, reducing demand for emergency public services, and ultimately saving or making better use of public dollars. Jacobson argues that evaluation of existing practice—for its cost-effectiveness with respect to corrections and other public system utilization—is critical, thus furthering the case for supporting evaluation research.

Attending to the needs of persons with histories of incarceration has become a more bipartisan issue, with the Bush Administration first providing $100 million in funds towards reentry initiatives in 2001 under the Severe and Violent Offender Reentry Initiative, and then providing a major impetus for action with Bush's call, in what would become known as the Prisoner Reentry Initiative, for allocating $300 million in funding towards reentry initiatives in his 2004 State of the Union Address. This was followed by the Second Chance Act, a bill that proposed allocating $100 million

over two years to help states address reentry issues and that narrowly missed passage by Congress in 2006. This bill represents a start, as considerably more resources would be needed to match the magnitude of the reentry problem. But such beginnings encourage hope that the policy atmosphere will be more open to addressing the needs of those released from jails and prisons now than it has been during the decades-long growth in the incarcerated population.

In the last several years there has also been increased policy emphasis on ending (as opposed to managing) homelessness. More than 200 communities around the country have recently committed themselves to 10-year plans to end homelessness (Interagency Council on Homelessness, 2006; Cunningham et al., 2006). A particular target for many of these plans is the "chronic" elements of this homeless population. "Chronically homeless" refers to persons who have been homeless for extended periods, often have one or more disabilities, and disproportionately use other public services and institutions, including jails and prisons. These plans to end homelessness are increasingly seeking to bypass emergency shelters and transitional housing, instead placing persons who are homeless directly into permanent housing with support services, when needed. Insofar as these renewed efforts at addressing homelessness have the capacity and the will to specifically respond to incarceration, this policy focus also promises to be receptive to ameliorating the nexus between homelessness and incarceration.

Both from the reentry and homelessness perspectives, there are grounds to believe that increased attention will be focused on addressing the nexus of incarceration and homelessness. This is, however, still an issue in its infancy. As such, there is a particular need for research that outlines the parameters of this problem and provides evidence for what approaches can effectively address this problem. It is these areas that provide the foci for this paper.

Synthesis of Research Literature: Findings and Discussion

Empirical Basis for Defining the Issue

The basis of the link between incarceration and homelessness is the degree to which there is overlap among the populations—whether it is measured from the perspective of the prevalence of homelessness among an incarcerated population or prevalence of incarceration among a homeless population. That a substantial overlap exists should not be surprising given the similarities in profiles between the incarcerated population and the single adult homeless population, where incarceration is most prevalent. Both are both predominantly male, young, and minority (Langan & Levin, 2002; Burt et al., 1999; Mauer, 1999; Culhane & Metraux, 1999). People in both populations are typically poor and undereducated and possess few job skills (Western & Beckett, 1999; Lichtenstein & Kroll, 1996; Burt et al., 1999). Both populations are characterized by the research literature and the mainstream media as having high rates of disability, especially involving mental illness and substance abuse (Burt et al., 1999; Freudenburg, 2001; Conklin et al., 2000; Lamb, 1998; Peters et al., 1998).

Experience of Homelessness Among the Prison Population

Prisons are run by state or federal government entities. In contrast to jails, prisons incarcerate persons who are convicted of more serious offenses and who serve considerably longer sentences. Prisons are typically located at considerable distances from where incarcerated individuals lived prior to their conviction. In 1999, the average time served for state prisoners was 34 months (Hughes, Wilson, & Beck, 2001), and in 2002 the average time served in federal prison (felony convictions) was 49 to 50 months (U.S. Sentencing Commission, 2004). Most persons are either released from prison on parole, meaning that the last part of their sentence is served while they are in the community and supervised by a

parole board, or are released without supervision after serving their full sentence in prison.

Lengthy periods of incarceration in remote locations often attenuate the social and family ties that are crucial for successful reentry into the community. Regained economic and residential stability almost always requires that a person receive, upon release from prison, support from family, social service agencies, faith-based organizations, or other parties interested in facilitating a smooth transition for the released individual. In the absence of such supports (and in some instances the absence of any type of effective discharge plan), individuals released from prison are at high risk for homelessness as well as other undesirable outcomes.

Only a handful of studies examine the overlap of prison and homelessness, and the extant literature has limited comparability due to variation in the study populations and the time frames used. However, taken together, the research suggests that about a tenth of the population coming into prisons have recently been homeless, and at least the same percentage of those who leave prisons end up homeless, for at least some period of time.

These studies include a Bureau of Justice Statistics (BJS) study (Hughes, Wilson, & Beck, 2001), which found that, among a nationwide survey of state prisoners expecting to be released in 1999, 12 percent reported being homeless at the time of their arrest. Another nationwide BJS study (Ditton, 1999) found that in 1998, 9 percent of state prison inmates reported living on the street or in a shelter in the 12 months prior to arrest. A California study (California Department of Corrections, 1997) reported that in 1997, 10 percent of the state's parolees were homeless. This study also found that in urban areas such as San Francisco and Los Angeles, an estimated 30–50 percent of all parolees were homeless. A 1999 Urban Institute three-site study of 400 returning prisoners with histories of drug abuse found that 32 percent had been homeless for a month or more at least once in their lifetimes, and 18 percent reported they were homeless for at least a month in the year after they were released from prison (Rossman et al.,

1999). The Massachusetts Housing and Shelter Alliance (Hombs, 2002) reported that 9.3 percent, 10.5 percent, and 6.3 percent of all people exiting state prisons in Massachusetts in 1997, 1998, and 1999, respectively, went directly to shelters after release. In The Urban Institute's four-site Returning Home study (Visher, 2006), anywhere from 2 percent (Maryland, Ohio, and Texas) to 5 percent (Illinois) of respondents slept at a shelter during their first night out of prison. Another 3 to 4 percent slept at a hotel, motel, or rooming house the first night out.

Research by Metraux and his colleagues used administrative data to not only assess shelter use among a cohort of persons released from state prisons, but also to assess factors associated with higher likelihoods of shelter use following release. Metraux and Culhane (2004), looking at people exiting the New York State prison system to New York City locations, found that, with incomplete pre-incarceration data, 6.6 percent had a history of shelter use in the two-year period prior to incarceration and, with more complete post-incarceration data, 11.4 percent had an episode of shelter use in the two-year period subsequent to release. Metraux (2007), looking at persons released from state prisons to Philadelphia locations, found the rate of shelter admissions within two years to be 4.3 percent. The later study found that a proxy measure for mental illness was associated with a substantial increase in the likelihood of a shelter stay. In both studies, an indicator of a history of shelter use prior to incarceration, although incomplete, was a strong predictor of subsequent shelter stay in both studies. Increasing age was also significantly linked to higher likelihoods of post-release shelter use (and decreasing likelihood of reincarceration) in both studies, suggesting that as persons "age out" of criminal activity their risk for homelessness increases. Finally, the studies showed conflicting results on the effect of parole on homelessness, with the New York study showing release on parole to increase the likelihood of shelter stay, while the Philadelphia study showed a significant decrease in this likelihood.

These two studies, which merge data from multiple and large administrative datasets and use multivariate regression methods to assess various factors and their associations with the likelihood of shelter use, go beyond simply reporting rates and permit some insight into risk factors for homelessness among persons released from prison. For example, both studies confirm that shelter use prior to prison entry is the strongest predictor of post-release shelter use, a finding that lends itself well to being incorporated into a simple screening mechanism for targeting persons at-risk for homelessness. However, more studies of this type of sophistication, using other types of data, are needed to build a base of evidence for the role of such key factors as mental illness or parole supervision on the risk for homelessness after release from prison.

Experience of Homelessness Among the Jail Population

In contrast to prisons, most people are in jail for lesser offenses and only for a short time—the median stay is one day. Quick release commonly occurs when persons post bail or serve minimal time for minor offenses or charges are dropped. People will stay in jail longer when they are unable to post bail and remain in jail while awaiting trial or, following conviction, when persons convicted for lesser offenses serve their remaining time in jail. Some defendants are given split sentences, which involve a period of probation supervision after jail time is completed.

Persons serving longer jail sentences may have similar reentry issues as their imprisoned counterparts. However, even short-term incarcerations may disrupt lives and interfere with the ability to maintain employment and housing. Few jails have pre-release programs that provide case management services to link prisoners leaving jail to community services (Steadman & Veysey, 1997) and/or housing. Those on probation may have a number of court-ordered probationary conditions that make it difficult to return to live with family or friends or to find appropriate housing. Probation clients mandated to find employment right after release may be pressured to find a job regardless of how far the job is from their

intended housing. While the housing options may be fewer given probation restrictions, being on probation may provide structured support to assist a released prisoner's search for housing.

The few studies on homelessness among jailed populations suggest that the rates of homelessness for those exiting jails are lower and more loosely coupled with the jail release than they are for those exiting prison. However, because the jail population is much larger that the prison population, the number of persons exiting jails who become homeless is much larger. Metraux and Culhane (2003) found that, among 76,111 persons released from New York City jails in 1997, 5.5 percent entered New York City shelters for single adults in the subsequent two-year period. A recent BJS survey of jail inmates (James & Glaze, 2006) found that for jail inmates without a mental heath problem, 9 percent reported homelessness in the year before jail entry, as compared to 17 percent of those who had a mental health problem. In a sample count of jail inmates in Salt Lake City in July 2005 and January 2006, nearly 10 percent identified themselves as homeless (Reentry Policy Council, 2006). One study of frequent jail users found that 82 percent of repeat users of jail in a metropolitan area in the South were transient or homeless at jail intake (Ford, 2005). McNiel, Binder, and Robinson (2005) looked at homelessness and mental illness among a jailed population. The study found that for the almost 13,000 jail episodes that were examined, in 16 percent of the episodes the person in question was homeless at the point of arrest, and in 18 percent of the episodes the person in question was diagnosed with a mental disorder. This rate of mental disorder was 30 percent among the episodes involving homelessness. Furthermore, homelessness and a "dual diagnosis" of severe mental disorder and substance-related disorders were associated with longer jail episodes.

As with examining prison to homelessness, the literature here is sparse and offers only a sketch of the nexus between jail and homelessness. The extent and dynamics here need further exploration and need to incorporate other dynamics such as was

done in the study by McNiel and colleagues. Furthermore, given that both homelessness and incarceration, especially in jails, disproportionately impact impoverished, minority males (Harrison & Beck, 2006; Culhane & Metraux, 1999), it is unclear how much more elevated the rates of homelessness are among persons released from jail when compared to a comparable group of persons who have not been jailed.

Experience of Incarceration Among the Homeless Population

Just as homelessness is a common experience among persons incarcerated in jails and prisons, having had an incarceration experience, be it jail or prison, is a common occurrence among single adults who are homeless. Conversely, the studies that examine incarceration histories among homeless populations are also difficult to compare, but judging from the results it appears that upwards of 20 percent of a single adult homeless population can be assumed to have been incarcerated at some point.

Examples of such studies include Metraux and Culhane's (2006) examination of a sheltered single adult population in New York City. In this study, 23.1 percent experienced at least one incarceration episode in the two-year period prior to the date examined. This included 7.7 percent with a prison stay and 17.0 percent with a jail stay. According to the 1996 National Survey of Homeless Assistance Providers and Clients (NSHAPC), 49 percent of homeless adults reported at least one lifetime experience of having spent five or more days in a city or county jail, 4 percent had spent time in a military lock-up, and 18 percent had been incarcerated in a state or federal prison (Burt et al., 1999). A recent study of 1,426 community-based homeless and marginally housed adults found that 23.1 percent of study participants had a history of imprisonment (Kushel et al., 2005). Schlay and Rossi's (1992) summary of twenty studies conducted in the 1980s found that, depending on the study, 4 percent to 49 percent of the homeless population report serving time in prison. The mean across the studies was 18 percent.

When focusing on persons diagnosed with mental illness, the intersections between homelessness and incarceration appear to be intensified (Metraux & Culhane, 2004; Ditton, 1999). In contrast, however, Solomon and Draine (1999) found more tenuous links between criminal justice history and homelessness in a sample of 325 psychiatric probation and parole clients. Other studies examining homelessness and criminal justice-related risk factors among persons with mental illness focus primarily on arrests, without examining incarceration specifically. Several studies here have found housing instability to be associated with an increased likelihood of coming into contact with police and of being charged with a criminal offense (Brekke et al., 2001; Clark, Ricketts, & McHugo, 1999; Martell, Rosner & Harmon, 1995). Metraux and Culhane (2006, 2004) also present evidence suggesting that the trajectories between homelessness and prison and homelessness and jail vary. The links between prison and homelessness are much more immediate, with an episode of homelessness being most likely to occur within 30 days of a prison release. This suggests that homelessness among persons released from prison is a reentry issue. This is consistent with research that shows persons released from prison to be at greatest risk for a variety of undesirable outcomes during this time period (Nelson, Deess, & Allen, 1999; Travis, Solomon, & Waul, 2001). Furthermore, Metraux and Culhane (2004) find that shelter use increases, albeit modestly, the risk for a subsequent reincarceration. In contrast, Metraux and Culhane (2006) found that shelter and jail use tended to follow a more sequential pattern featuring multiple stays in each system and a more prolonged pattern of residential instability.

The Research Evidence: What Do We Know?
Evidence collected so far supports perceptions that there is a tangible link between incarceration and homelessness. However, most of the evidence linking incarceration and homelessness is correlational, and cannot demonstrate that incarceration causes increased risk for homelessness, or vice versa. While there is a

need for studies that are capable of assessing causality in this relationship, the associations demonstrated here in the high rates of homelessness among incarcerated populations, and the high rates of incarceration among homeless populations, are consistent with other bodies of research that highlight factors which explain why such high rates would exist. The research reviewed here documents specific and multiple barriers to housing among persons recently released from carceral institutions, and increased vulnerability for arrest and incarceration among homeless persons. This research not only supplies explanations for the high rates just reported, it also implies that addressing these factors could ameliorate the connections between homelessness and incarceration.

Barriers to Housing for Persons Who Have Been Incarcerated
There are structural as well as individual barriers to housing for soon-to-be-released prisoners. These barriers start even before release. For example, one fundamental obstacle to effective discharge planning in prison is that prisons tend to be located in rural areas, whereas most persons released from prison will return to urban areas hundreds of miles from the prison where they were incarcerated. This geographic mismatch renders it difficult to connect returning prisoners to the available housing market or for discharge staff and social workers to even attempt to provide housing assistance, as they are unlikely to have sufficient knowledge of the housing landscape to aid returning prisoners.

Oftentimes, however there will not even be adequate discharge planning and other support services available to incarcerated persons prior to their release. Survey data for state prison inmates from 1997 reveal that only 13 percent of soon-to-be-released inmates reported participating in pre-release programs (Lynch & Sabol, 2001). Most likely, an even smaller percentage receives housing-related assistance (e.g., counseling, search assistance, referrals to local housing providers, vouchers for rent, renter education, etc.) within these programs. An Urban Institute study tracking released prisoners in Illinois found that of clients who

responded that they "did not have a place to live lined up" upon release, only 21 percent participated in pre-release programs. Of those who did participate in pre-release programs, almost half (45 percent) reported that finding a place to live was not covered in the program. In addition, for those who discussed finding housing in their program, only 39 percent received housing referral information (LaVigne et al., 2003). These numbers were similar to the findings of reentry studies in Ohio and Texas (Visher 2006; Visher & Courtney, 2006). The findings suggest that discharge planning involving the provision of housing-related services is rarely a standard part of the pre-release suite of services.

[...]

Fees and Fines Don't Allow the Homeless to Catch Up

Terrell Jermaine Starr

Terrell Jermaine Starr is a senior editor at AlterNet, an award-winning news magazine that covers a wide variety of topics, including human rights, social justice, health care issues, and more.

The criminalization of America's poor has been quietly gaining steam for years, but a recent study, "The Poor Get Prison" co-authored by Karen Dolan and Jodi L. Carr, reveals the startling extent to which American municipalities are fining and jailing the country's most vulnerable people, not just punishing them for being poor, but driving them deeper into poverty.

"In the last ten years," Barbara Ehrenreich writes in the introduction, "it has become apparent that being poor is in itself a crime in many cities and counties, and that it is a crime punished by further impoverishment."

A few months ago, the Department of Justice's Ferguson report revealed how that city has disproportionately targeted its majority minority population with traffic and other minor infractions that heavily support the municipality's coffers. But Ferguson is far from alone. Municipalities like New York City have greatly increased the number of minor offenses that are considered criminal (like putting your feet up in the subway) or sitting on the sidewalk. Wealthy white people in business attire are rarely targeted for such summonses, and if they are, they can quickly pay the fine or hire counsel to get out of it. The over-punishment of minor offenses is just another way the rich get richer, and as the report says, the "poor get prison." They also get poorer and more numerous. In one striking statistic, the Southern Educational Foundation reports that 51 percent of America's public schoolchildren are living in poverty.

Perversely, it is the poor who, according to Dolan and Carr, are subsidizing municipalities' budgets and becoming reliable sources of enrichment for the private companies contracted by local governments to carry out what used to be government duties.

Here are five troubling trends from the report that show us how the government is financially abusing poor people.

1. Jailing probationers who can't pay fees and fines

More than four million people are sentenced to probation in America, according to the report. Because state funding for probation services is on the decline, more private companies are talking over the responsibility of managing them. Private probation companies don't charge local governments for their services, so there is no fee to the taxpayer. Probationers, however, are charged a supervision fee, and if they can't afford to pay, they face jail time. Despite the fact that it is unconstitutional to jail people because they can't pay fines, the reality is that many probationers are poor and unaware of their rights and they end up in modern-day debtors' prisons.

"While indigent people have a right to free counsel in some cases, more municipalities are requiring an 'application fee' of at least $50 to pay for a public defender," Karen Dolan, a co-author of the study, told AlterNet via email. "Many poor people with misdemeanor charges end up before a judge without legal representation and do not understand their rights. Without legal representation, poor people often don't understand that they ought not to be offered 'jail or probation' simply for debt, and they choose probation. They unwittingly enter into a potential dungeon of debt due to the huge fees charged by private probation companies and inability to pay those eventually—illegally—leads to jail anyway."

At least 13 states allow localities to outsource probation supervision services. In 2012, these companies generated $100 million in revenue.

2. Taking poor people's property through asset forfeit seizures

More than $3 billion in cash and property has been seized by local and state police agencies through a Department of Justice asset seizure program. Eighty percent of the assets collected through this program stay with the law enforcement agencies that collect them, the *Washington Post* reported. Under asset forfeit seizure programs, cops can take someone's property simply under "reasonable suspicion" it was used to commit a crime; the burden of proof is on the property owner that the seizure was unjustified.

Dolan and Carr's report outlines how this program disproportionately impacts the poor, especially black and Latino people. Given that black and Latino working families are twice as likely as whites to be low-income, they are less likely to have the financial resources to reclaim property that was, in many cases, wrongfully taken from them.

3. School-to-prison pipeline

Black students make up just 16 percent of the population but represent 32-42 percent of students who are suspended or expelled, according to the "The Poor Get Prison" report. Many school districts around the country use local police to provide security, which further increases these students' chances of arrest.

"When you have zero tolerance policies, combined with law enforcement officers at the doors and in the hallways and you have a poor and black student body—both demographics considered potential criminals from the time they board the bus in the morning—you have the makings of unnecessarily harsh and punitive actions against black students," Dolan told AlterNet.

"Studies show that students with disabilities are also disproportionately affected by overly harsh punishments at school," she continued. "The two overriding factors appear to be class and race. Poverty plays a big role, but overlaying that is what seems only explainable by a widespread cultural bias against black youth, especially black male youth, even small children who are black

and poor. The presumption that black schoolchildren are potential criminals seems to play into the disparity in the levels and severity of discipline when you compare them with white schoolchildren."

As previous studies have shown, people with arrest records find it difficult to find employment. A 2013 National Institute of Justice report cited a study that was carried out in New York City that found people with a criminal record are 50 percent less likely to get a call back for a job interview; most of those affected are black.

What this tells us is that the criminalization of poor black and Latino children through hyper-disciplinary actions doesn't end at the schoolhouse door. It is a poverty-inducing policy that harms these kids' employability prospects later in life.

4. Hyper criminalization of petty infractions

The New York City Council is considering proposals to make petty crimes like peeing in public and drinking from an open container civil instead of criminal offenses. This follows years of hyper-policing and criminalizing an increasing list of tiny infractions.

Since 2001, 81 percent of the people fined and punished under these "broken windows" policing policies have been Latinos or black Americans, many them from the city's poorest communities.

New York is not alone in its enforcement of petty violations. In Ferguson, for example, revenue from its police department enforcing municipal codes were expected to account for 23 percent of the city's budget or more than $3 million. In 2013, that figure was $2.46 million.

Loistine Hoskin, a resident of Ferguson, told CNN that her car was towed in 2009 because it was missing a tire. She chose to pay a $1,200 fine rather than try to fight the ticket in court and face the threat of jail, she said.

"It's definitely a vicious cycle," Hoskin, 64, a retired airline reservation agent, told CNN. "Unfortunately for most people who are in this cycle, they continue to be in a downward spiral because they can't get jobs, they can't do anything, they can't pay the fines."

5. Fining the homeless for being homeless.

If you are homeless in America and have nowhere to go and are down on your luck, it is increasingly difficult to find a safe space in which to exist without being fined for loitering. According to the report, an estimated 600,000 people are homeless on any given night. Though nearly 13 percent of the nation's low-income housing has been lost since 2001, and many people simply cannot afford housing, 34 percent of cities ban public camping, 18 percent prohibit sleeping in public and 43 percent prevent people from sleeping in vehicles, according to a study the report cited.

Often, homeless people who are fined for violating these laws have no way to pay the fine. Jailtime is on the table for many who can't pay up.

One example of how economically devastating these fines are comes out of Missouri. Edward Brown, 62 and homeless, has been jailed at least twice since 2009 for failing to pay fines, one of which stems from his failure to get a rabies vaccination for his dog, Matrix. He was ticketed $464 and just barely paid it off. Brown's monthly Social Security check is $484.

The report offers suggestions for addressing some of these issues. Whether those in power will listen to the solutions is another matter.

When asked whether race or poverty was the factor driving the criminalization of the poor, Dolan said the two are intertwined.

"I don't think we can separate the two," she said. "It's not an either/or. It's a both/and. There's no question that poor people of all races are vastly more impacted by fines, fees, aggressive policing and more vulnerable in court than people with the ability to pay misdemeanor charges and afford legal representation. And there is no question that the mandate for police and court systems to fill in budget deficits by aggressive collection of these fines are more prevalent in lower-income areas, regardless of race.

"But there is equally no question that racial profiling has been ever-present in our country despite civil rights laws designed to address such bias and discrimination. And black people are

disproportionately poor and disproportionately policed and incarcerated in this country. Police and courts in low-income/high poverty areas are increasingly in the service of aggressive money collection rather than public safety. When racist bias is added to this already fraught situation, the match is thrown on this tinderbox and consequences can be deadly."

Poverty and the Criminal Justice System Go Hand in Hand

Political Research Associates

Started in 1981, the Political Research Associates (PRA) have provided investigative research and information on America's right to social justice.

The police harassment of homeless people, criminalization of behaviors that stem from poverty, and unfair targeting of poor neighborhoods: the criminal justice system targets and harasses poor and homeless people. The working class and the poor (people working and out of work) are stigmatized, scapegoated, and mistreated by the criminal justice system. Those unable to afford an attorney often find themselves represented by underresourced, inadequate and irresponsible public defenders, and are unable to adequately defend themselves in court. In addition, the poor may suffer further when public assistance is cut off because of a convicted spouse or family member.

Most People Who Interact with the Criminal Justice System Are Poor

- In 1991, more than half of all state prisoners reported an annual income of less than $10,000 prior to their arrest.[1]
- While roughly 80% of all U.S. men of working age are employed full-time, only 55% of state prison inmates were working full-time at the time of their arrest.[2]
- Only 33% of prisoners nationwide have completed high school, while in the general population 85% of all men 20 to 29 years old have a high school diploma.[3]

"Poverty and the Criminal Justice System," Political Research Associates, May, 2005. politicalresearch.org. Reprinted by permission.

- The United States spend $167 billion dollars on policing, corrections, judicial and legal services in 20014 and only $29.7 Billion on Temporary Aid to Needy Families (TANF)[5].

The Poor Are Increasingly Criminalized to Protect the Interest of the Wealthy

- The homeless are denied access to public space. More and more public parks are refusing entry to individual without children; public money is used to place bars in the middle of park benches to stop people from sleeping on them, and homeless people are being banned completely from certain neighborhoods in cities like Athens, Georgia; Cincinnati, Ohio; and Portland, Oregon.[6]
- The homeless are denied access to private space. Local businesses often band to form "Business Improvement Districts", organizations created in order to protect the interests of local businesses. The interests of these "Business Improvement Districts" are generally related to the eradication of the homeless presence in their area and often hire private security guards to restrict access to areas of the community based on economic profiling.[7]

The Rich Have Crucial Advantages in the Court System

- People that can afford bail are able to leave jail and conduct investigations, leaving them better prepared for trial. Higher-income people can afford better attorneys, expert witnesses, private detectives, and more "respectable" alibis.[8]
- People who can afford to hire an attorney are less likely to be imprisoned. Of the cases in which the defendant was found guilty in federal courts, 88% of defendants with a public attorney received prison sentences, compared to 77% of defendants with private lawyers, between 1990 and 1998.

In state courts, public and private attorney have similar prison sentence rates.[9]

- Those who cannot afford bail and come to the court from jail for their trial are more likely to be imprisoned. Between 1990 and 1998, in the 75 largest counties in the U.S., roughly 50% of felony defendants with a public lawyer or court assigned counsel were released from jail pending trail while approximately 75% of private lawyers were released.[10] The poor face harsher sentences simply because they cannot afford adequate legal assistance. The United States allots just $2.25 per person for civil legal assistance.11 England allocates $32, New Zealand $12, and Ontario $11.40.[12]

- Public defenders are overworked. Felony caseloads of 500, 600, 800 or more annually are common for many public defenders, although it is recommended that the annual caseload for a public defender should not exceed 150 felonies, 400 misdemeanors or 200 juvenile cases. For example, public defenders in Philadelphia were handling between 600 and 1,100 cases per year.[13] Because public defenders are overworked, it is not surprising that they win dismissals or acquittals less often than privately hired attorneys.

- Some defendants who cannot afford to hire an attorney themselves are never assigned a public defender. In 2002 there were more than 12,000 guilty pleas entered by people who were not represented by an attorney just in California alone.[14] Counties in Georgia have faced lawsuits after completely failing to provide counsel to misdemeanor defendants, or delaying so long to appoint counsel that the pretrial wait in jail was longer than the sentence would have been if a conviction had occurred.[15] Elsewhere, suspects are coerced into waiving their constitutional right to counsel in return for a 'deal,' available only if they plead guilty immediately. Very few jurisdictions comply with the U.S. Supreme Court's decision to extend the right to counsel to people receiving probation or a suspended sentence.[16]

- Many death row prisoners have been represented by incompetent and incapable lawyers or in some cases no lawyers at all. In Texas, about 1 in 4 death row prisoners was represented by a lawyer who at some point had been reprimanded, suspended, placed on probation, or barred from practicing law in Texas. The same is true for 1 in 5 prisoners that have faced execution in the past 20 years in Washington State. In Alabama, about 40 of the 185 death row prisoners do not have attorneys.17 A study by the Innocence Project of Cardozo Law School indicated that in 70 exonerated death row sentences, 32% of these cases occurred because of incompetent lawyers.[18]

Though Prisons Are Economically Detrimental to Communities, Prisons Are Pawned off on Poor Communities as Economic Miracles

- Public officials portray prisons as "clean industries" and promise new jobs to poor communities. However, prisons are often sited the same way other polluting industries are – focusing on poor communities of color. Prisons use large amounts of local natural resources, and towns where prisons are located are required to pay for the roads, sewers and utilities used by the prisons. Prison construction often takes land out of productive use.[19]
- Prison jobs typically do not go to residents of the host towns, and employees of the prisons rarely move into town after being hired. Since, the majority of prison employees commute to work, the host towns' local businesses see little, if any, business from the prison employees.[20]

Prison Stigmatizes People and Keeps Them in Poverty

- Ex-prisoners may be ineligible for welfare benefits.[21] Released prisoners may be barred from receiving Temporary Assistance to Needy Families, Social Security, Food Stamps, and other welfare benefits. Such benefits may be necessary for ex-prisoners who are newly released and trying to support themselves.

- Welfare Reform permanently banned anyone with a felony drug conviction (using or selling drugs) from receiving cash benefits or food stamps. No other felony convictions or offenses result in a permanent loss of these benefits. Each state can "opt out" of enforcing this ban, or modify its enforcement. As of December 2001, [22] states still have the full ban in place – denying people with felony drug convictions benefits for life.[22] Eight states and the District of Columbia have completely opted out of the ban, and 20 other states have modified the ban by either allowing benefits dependent upon drug treatment, denying people benefits only for sale convictions, or placing a time limit on the ban.[23]

- Much needed education is denied to anyone convicted of a drug related crime. In 1998 the Higher Education Act was amended to deny anyone with a drug conviction from receiving federal financial aid for post-secondary education.[24] Those with non-drug offenses, such as murder or rape, are eligible under this law. A student who has been convicted of any offense under any federal or state law involving the possession or sale of a controlled substance is not eligible to receive any grant, loan or work assistance if the money will be used to attend college. To date, approximately 92,841 students have been denied access to financial aid because of this provision.[25]

- Former prisoners have a sigma attached to incarceration and often have a difficult time obtaining work after release.

A researcher has estimates that the "wage penalty" of incarnation lowers the market rate of a prisoner's wage by 10 to 20 percent.[26]

Endnotes

1 USDOJ, Bureau of Justice Statistics, 1995. Survey of State Prison Inmates, 1991. http://www.ojp.usdoj.gov/bjs/pub/ascii/sospi91.txt (May 24, 2005).

2 Ibid

3 Ibid

4 Drug Policy Alliance. 2004. "U.S. Prison, Police Spending at Record Level" . See <http://www.drugpolicy.org/news/05_03_04bjs.cfm> (June 23, 2004).

5 National Conference of State Legislatures. 2002. "State to State TANF Spending, 2001". See <http://www.ncsl.org/statefed/welfare/state_spending01.htm> (June 23, 2004).

6 National Coalition for the Homeless. No Date. "Illegal to Be Homeless: The Criminalization of Homelessness in the United States," (Online). See <http://www.nationalhomeless.org/crimreport/executivesummary.html> (June 16, 2004).

7 Ibid P.4

8 Herzing, Rachel. 2005. "What is the Prison Industrial Complex?" See <http://www.defendingjustice.org>

9 U.S. Department of Justice, BJS, 2000. "Defense Counsel in Criminal Cases" See <http://www.ojp.usdoj.gov/bjs/pub/ascii/dccc.txt> (June 16, 2004).

10 U.S. Department of Justice, BJS, 2000. "Defense Counsel in Criminal Cases" See <http://www.ojp.usdoj.gov/bjs/pub/ascii/dccc.txt> (June 16, 2004).

11 Earl Johnson, Equal Access to Justice: Comparing Access to Justice in the United States and Other Industrial Democracies 24 Fordham Int'l L. J. 83 (2001).

12 Houseman, Alan W. , June 2001. "Recent Developments: Civil Legal Assistance in the United States," See <http://www.clasp.org/DMS/Documents/1011204465.21/recent%20developments.pdf> (June 23, 2004).

13 American Civil Liberties Union. "Rights of the Poor" See < http://www.aclu.org/poorrights/poorrightsmain.cfm> (June 16, 2004).

14 NLADA. 2003. "Five Problems Facing Public Defense on the 40th Anniversary of Gideon v. Wainwright," See <http://www.nlada.org/Defender/Defender_Gideon/Defender_Gideon_5_Problems> (June 17 2004).

15 Ibid P.1

16 Ibid P.1

17 Death Penalty Information Center. 2003. Understanding Capital Punishment: A Guide Through the Death Penalty Debate. Washington D.C. P 59.

18 The Innocence Project. 2001. Cases and Remedies of Wrongful Correction. See <http://www.innocenceproject.org/causes/index.php> (June 17, 2004).

19 United Church of Christ Commission for Racial Justice. 1987. Toxic Wastes and Race in the United States: A National Report On The Racial and Socioeconomic Characteristics of Communities With Hazardous Waste Sites. New York: Public Data Access, Inc.

20 King, Ryan S., Marc Mauer, and Tracy Huling, 2003. "Big Prisons, Small Towns: Prison Economies in Rural America." See <www.sentencingproject.org/pdfs/9037.pdf> (June 30, 2004).

21 Applied Research Center. 2002. From Poverty to Punishment. Oakland, CA: Applied Research Center.

22 Allard, Patricia. 2002. The Sentencing Project. "Life Sentences: Denying Welfare Benefits To Women Convicted Of Drug Offenses." See <http://www.sentencingproject.org>.

23 Ibid.

24 Ibid

25 Ibid

Homeless People Are More Susceptible to Public Order Offenses

Sydney Criminal Lawyers

Based in Sydney, Australia, the Sydney Criminal Lawyers specialize in criminal and traffic law.

Around 105,000 people are experiencing homelessness or housing stress in Australia – with Streetsmart estimating that 1 in 200 of us won't have a home to go to tonight.

The experience of homelessness has both long-term and wide-ranging consequences, often leading to contact with the criminal justice system.

Homelessness and Crime

Homelessness is recognised as a factor which often lead to criminal behaviour, yet we know surprisingly little about the link between homelessness and crime in Australia.

Research suggests many homeless people have had histories of violent or sexual abuse. But sadly, public policy often treats homeless people as perpetrators of crime, rather than victims.

Victims or Criminals?

Although there is often a link between homelessness and crime, there are complex factors that impact upon whether a particular person turns to crime. People often become involved in "survival crime" after becoming homeless, committing property offences to support themselves.

To further complicate the picture, a lifetime of trauma leading to homelessness and living a vulnerable life on the streets makes people more prone to substance abuse and mental health problems.

"Violent Cycles: Homelessness and Crimes," by Sydney Criminal Lawyers, Sydney Criminal Lawyers, January 27, 2016. Reprinted by permission.

The Australian Institute of Criminology's (AIC) Drug Use Monitoring in Australia program (DUMA) has been recording information relating to homelessness since 1999. The early data shows that a whopping one in ten people apprehended by police were homeless at the time of arrest.

DUMA recently expanded its survey to capture a broader view of homelessness, including housing stress. This suggests that massive 22 per cent of police detainees were experiencing homelessness prior to arrest.

The study also found that around one in ten police detainees are not confident they will have anywhere to live when once released, which minimises the impact of any rehabilitation services they may have been connected with as a result of arrest.

The AIC drew on these results to conduct groundbreaking research examining the factors underlying homelessness among Australian police detainees. It found a diversity range of reasons for homelessness, and that an individual, tailored approach to address underlying issues is important in reducing crime.

Dr. Catherine Robson's report Rough Living: Surviving Violence and Homelessness explores the experiences of six men and six women through a series of in-depth interviews over a three-month period. She concludes that despite common perceptions of homeless people as drug addicted criminals, people who are homeless are far more likely to be victims of crime than perpetrators.

Wide Ranging Issue

Homelessness affects people of all ages and backgrounds. Those living with mental illness or disability, Aboriginal and Torres Strait Islander peoples, the LGBTI community, and people leaving prison are most vulnerable.

And the Australian Human Rights Commission reports that the number of families with children and older women reaching out to homelessness services is steadily increasing.

Homelessness and Crime

The AIC's findings suggest that a disproportionate number of homeless people have a criminal history, their crimes are normally less-serious in nature.

Living in public spaces, people who are homeless are more susceptible to committing public order offences like trespassing and public urination.

Those struggling to survive living rough often report they have no choice but to participate in crimes like shoplifting and squatting, and that they have always used drugs to cope with trauma, which leads them to commit other crimes to support their addiction.

The AIC's study acknowledges that "police may specifically target homeless populations because of perceived community safety issues, or because homeless populations are more visible to street policing operations."

Those who were arrested and reported experiencing homeless had a range of reasons for becoming homeless in the first place. From most common to least common, their answers were:

- Family/relationship breakdown
- Financial circumstances/job loss
- Drug problem
- Property eviction
- Court or justice order
- Alcohol problem
- Domestic violence
- Lack of family or social support/death of a family member
- Recent arrival (no means of support)
- Mental health problem
- Gambling problem
- Can't explain

They described varied living situations for the 30 days prior to their arrest, including:

- Living in someone else's house or apartment temporarily
- Shelter or emergency housing
- Prison
- Halfway house
- Drug or alcohol treatment program
- Hospital or psychiatric hospital
- On the street with no fixed address
- Long grass

Homeless and Non-Homeless Offenders

The AIC's data suggests that there are important differences between homeless and non-homeless people arrested by police.

While over 80 per cent of people detained by police are male, for people who are homeless, the gender balance is roughly half/half. Homeless detainees were found to be a little older, more likely to have had a history of criminal behaviour, and more likely to test positive for drugs when arrested.

Two thirds were reported to have been drinking alcohol prior to their arrest.

Addressing Underlying Issues

Around half of Sydney's homeless are likely to have been a victim of violence in the last year.

Australian Bureau of Statistics figures suggest that only 5 per cent of people living in NSW with stable accommodation reported experiencing violence within the same time frame.

In the context of a traumatic home life followed by a dangerous life on the street, it is possible to see how homeless people become involved in crime.

Addressing the underlying issues that lead to homelessness – including sexual trauma, drug and alcohol abuse, and various mental health issues – and providing housing support to these vulnerable people is crucial to reducing rates of crime, which ultimately benefits the whole community.

Homelessness Being a Crime Is the Real Crime

Allen Arthur

Allen Arthur is a writer for SocialistWorker.org, covering topics such as politics, social justice, human rights, and more.

O n a recent Monday afternoon at the corner of 29th Street and Park Avenue in the high-end Murray Hill neighborhood of Manhattan, two middle-aged men sat in the shade of a phone booth.

While they met there often, asking for change or chatting, on this day, they were approached by the NYPD's Homeless Services. Four armbanded officers with guns emerged from marked and unmarked vans to move the men away from the corner.

Scenes like this happen every day in every city. If it seems like an encounter with police is the last thing homeless people need, that is exactly what they face. As affordable housing options decrease, social services go underfunded, and the activities of homeless people and their advocates are further criminalized, homeless populations are being tossed into more frequent interactions with police.

These interactions not only highlight the diminishing options for the poorest and most vulnerable people in the U.S., but they have steadily become more deadly. Amid the wave of high-profile police brutality cases galvanizing the country, several involve the deaths of homeless people.

Brendon Glenn was an unarmed black man and father of a new baby boy who was said by friends to have been struggling with alcohol. In May, he was murdered by police in Venice Beach after having an argument with a bouncer.

In the Miami neighborhood of Overtown Park, police killed an unnamed man in June for refusing to drop a pipe. The shooting occurred in front of a YMCA, with multiple children witnessing it.

"Homelessness is the crime, not the homeless," by Allen Arthur, Socialist Worker.org, August 19, 2015. Reprinted by permission.

Albuquerque--where the police murder rate is double Chicago's and eight times that of New York City--recently awarded $5 million to the family of James Boyd, a diagnosed schizophrenic living in the mountains, who police attempted to remove for "camping illegally." With Boyd armed with two large knives, the resulting standoff, involving more than 40 officers, lasted over four hours. When Boyd finally went to put the knives down, the cops opened fire.

Perhaps the best known of these incidents is that of Charly Keunang, better known as Africa.

A resident of Los Angeles' Skid Row, Keunang was an immigrant who struggled with depression and addiction. On the morning of March 1, officers roused Keunang from his tent. During the ensuing confrontation, one cop erroneously claimed that Keunang grabbed his gun--officers then shot Keunang six times. The LAPD refused to release body camera footage, but a bystander filmed the murder. Upon that video's release, the LAPD and local media joined forces for a massive smear campaign, dredging up Keunang's criminal past to justify his murder.

A recent and powerful article in GQ has brought this story some needed publicity, and his family recently filed a lawsuit against the city, the officers and LAPD Chief Charlie Beck.

While the murders have grabbed the most attention, their backdrop has been a massive criminalization of homelessness. Dozens of cities have passed "food sharing bans." Last summer, the NYPD conducted a series of raids on homeless shelters on the otherwise white and wealthy Upper West Side.

These punitive policies have been particularly prevalent in the U.S., but we are not alone: London has even put down spikes in areas where the homeless frequently sleep. The spikes are called--seriously--"defensive architecture."

The National Law Center on Homelessness and Poverty recently released a scathing report entitled No Safe Place. Examining the trend of criminalization, researchers found a number of startling facts: nearly one-fifth of all U.S. cities have a ban on sleeping in public; one-quarter have banned begging in public; and 43 percent

of cities have banned sleeping in vehicles. The report also makes note of the many cities that enforce such bans--yet don't provide adequate shelter facilities for the homeless.

Pointing to numerous studies that showed housing and social workers to be vastly more cost-effective than police presence in dealing with homelessness, No Safe Place quotes the CEO of the Central Florida Commission on Homelessness:

The law enforcement costs alone are ridiculous. They're out of control...Our community will spend nearly half a billion dollars and at the end of the decade, these people will still be homeless. It doesn't make moral sense, and now we know it doesn't make financial sense.

All of the victims of police murder mentioned above were also struggling with addiction or mental illness--but, of course, poor communities and communities of color have unequal access to health resources (both mental and physical) and rehabilitation. Even federal funding for job training has decreased.

All of this has built a seemingly impenetrable wall around the homeless--and the police have been unleashed, as Keeanga-Yamhatta Taylor put it during a talk at the Socialism 2015 conference, to manage the erosion of social services.

Unsurprisingly, the populations most affected by homelessness are those that usually bear the brunt of society's violence.

Over 40 percent of homeless people in the U.S. are Black. More than a quarter are Latino. The Williams Institute reports that a staggering 40 percent of homeless youth identify as LGBTQ. Around 12 percent of homeless are veterans--their job deified when wartime profits call, but left for dead in the streets when their usefulness is exhausted.

It should also be noted that nearly a third of those living in New York City homeless shelters are employed--at jobs that obviously don't pay them enough to afford rent.

Stagnant or dropping wages, closures of schools and hospitals, wide-scale unemployment and slashed benefits drive many of the homeless to illegal means, just so they can eat. Drug use and sales,

theft and even "survival sex"--prostitution not for money, but in exchange for the most basic necessities, such as food or a shower-- are some of the too-common ways that the homeless attempt to make it on the streets.

In the absence of suitable facilities and resources for the homeless, politicians hoping to appear "tough on crime" or desperate to cater to wealthy property owners use stories about these underground survival economies as an excuse to brutalize and criminalize the homeless.

But the dirty secret about homelessness is that, with an estimated 600,000 people homeless at any given moment and over 3 million homeless annually, the U.S. has about 18 million empty homes.

Despite the politicians' claims, it isn't true that the resources aren't available to adequately fight homelessness. On the contrary, in New York City, which has an astounding 10 percent of the country's homeless population, Mayor Bill de Blasio agreed to spend nearly $170 million on 1,300 new police officers, but hasn't created any viable affordable housing program to counter the mass displacement taking place, nor provided any substantial new funding for the city's underserved shelters.

The city's prisons, including the notorious Rikers Island, spend over $96,000 per year per prisoner, enough to give each one a home at the average New York City rent for nearly three years. Meanwhile, Los Angeles, which has about 5 percent of the country's homeless, has labeled Skid Row a "police containment zone" and assigned a cop for every block.

Back in New York, de Blasio's plan to "save public housing" depends almost entirely on incentives for private developers. Far from building housing as a public good, the plan ignores de Blasio's central campaign promise to raise taxes on the wealthiest New Yorkers--a promise which helped get him elected in a landslide- -and instead raises fees on working people, operating on the model that if the developers don't make millions as a precondition, nothing will get done.

While conservative critics in the *New York Post* and elsewhere decry the mayor's supposedly liberal failures, de Blasio's policies are largely continuations of his Republican predecessors Rudy Giuliani and Michael Bloomberg.

The de Blasio administration has recently come under fire for the horrific conditions at private homeless shelters receiving city contracts. Slumlords are paid as much as $3,000 per month per apartment by the city to operate buildings that have been cited for mold, collapsing structures and vermin--and which are held to virtually zero oversight.

If there is sufficient money to help the homeless and it's cheaper to help poor people than to lock them away, why don't the politicians simply end homelessness?

Because there's no profit in it. Real estate developers donate massive amounts of money to politicians to not find adequate housing for everyone--and also to maximize the profitability of both existing housing and clear the way for new developments. Even when affordable housing is worked in, the developers are enticed not by altruism, but by tax breaks.

Similarly, by criminalizing the homeless, politicians are able to stoke racist and xenophobic fear, perpetuating the idea that "lazy" or "criminal" populations don't deserve help toward obtaining suitable, humane housing--but instead should be dealt with as an unfortunate element that endangers a city's quality of life. Both politically and economically, for the ruling class, the problem is more profitable than the solution.

While the statistics and the grisly cycles they illustrate seem insurmountable, there is a simple solution: make housing a human right for all people.

Eighteen million homes sit empty not because we have no one to fill them, but because they are kept empty for the sake of profit. As the news touts a recovery in new home construction, millions of people still live without homes or teeter just on the edge of housing insecurity, one unexpected expense away from being kicked out on the street.

Once there, they won't be offered raises, trained in new skills or have access to fully funded shelters to assist in the journey back to stability. Instead, cities are offering a jail cell as their only housing plan. It isn't some fundamental misunderstanding about how to treat the homeless, but the prioritization of wealth over their well-being that keeps so many people on the streets.

Untreated Mental Illness Is a Gateway to Homelessness

Eve Abrams

Eve Abrams currently teaches writing at the Waldo Burton School and is also a radio producer, writer, and audio documentarian, having also taught in public and charter schools in New Orleans and New York City.

Our ongoing series Unprisoned has been bringing you stories of how mass incarceration affects New Orleans.

Last time, we learned about New Orleans Municipal Court, the largest criminal court in Louisiana. Today, we follow Municipal Court to the New Orleans Mission — where a large number of homeless people who are facing municipal charges are being served directly.

Leroy Perry is the Re-Entry Coordinator at the New Orleans Mission, one of the city's largest homeless shelters. A week before Municipal Court came to the New Orleans Mission, Perry points to the corner of the Mission's Transitional House.

"The judge sits right here in his robe, and he sets up just like he would in the courtroom with his clerk and everybody right here," Perry says. "He even has his nameplate. It's just like court here."

To understand why Louisiana's highest volume criminal court holds sessions at a homeless shelter is to understand how intertwined the criminal justice system has become with homelessness in New Orleans.

"A lot of the people that are homeless, and hang around here and come here for our services, they have legal problems hanging over their head — that if they can't get to, they're afraid to get to," Perry says. "And this is very reassuring to them. Because the judge

"With so many homeless caught up in the criminal justice system, New Orleans holds court at a shelter," by Eve Abrams, New Orleans Public Radio, WWNO, Feb 03, 2016. Reprinted by permission.

comes here, and we let them know: we're not trying to take anybody to jail. We're trying to get your problem resolved, and that's what they do: they bring them here and get it resolved."

People who come through this system are poor.

Brandi Studer is the social worker for the Orleans Parish Defenders in Municipal Court. People who work at the court call it Muni. "People who come through this system are poor," says Studer.

Orleans Parish Defenders, or OPD, represent around 85 percent of the people arrested in Orleans Parish. Which means approximately 85 percent of people arrested are at or below the poverty level. Studer's job is to keep these clients out of jail by getting them back into school or into a substance abuse program, or maybe a bed. Whatever each person needs.

"A lot of our clients come because they were panhandling, or they have a mental illness crisis in public and the cops don't know what else to do with them but to arrest them, or their families don't know what else to do but call the cops," says Studer. "And then they end up in the system, they end up spending a couple days in jail and getting court costs and fines and fees."

Which are hard to pay when you don't have a job, never mind a reliable place to sleep. The Orleans Parish Defenders estimate that at least one-quarter of their Municipal Court clients are homeless, and at least one-third suffer with some level of mental illness. The numbers are so high, Muni holds three specialized courts: mental health, human trafficking and homeless court.

Most often, the homeless are charged with public intoxication, obstruction of a public passageway (often from sleeping), or trespassing (often, sleeping in an abandoned building). Some people are arrested so frequently, the judges know them by sight. Public Defender Lauren Anderson has one client who has been arrested 186 times.

"But these aren't people who are walking around with iPhones and calendars," says Anderson. "Some of them don't even know where they are, what day of the week it is. So remembering that 'I need to be in Section B of Municipal Court a month-and-a-half

from now' is just impossible, and they'll say things to us like, 'Well, I remember getting this ticket from this officer, but then one day it rained and my ticket got wet.' And people don't believe that, but that is an actual thing that happens. These are people who are sleeping under bridges."

A ticket, or summons, from a police officer, or a subpoena from the court, is a sheet of paper, and pretty much the only way someone knows when to appear in court. You can call the clerk of court, but if you don't know what section you're in and call the wrong clerk, or your name was spelled incorrectly in the system, or your birthday is off, chances are, no one will find your case.

"I was in court one day when a judge said: 'Put the papers under your pillow, and that way you won't lose them,'" recalls Brandi Studer. "And the girl goes, 'I don't have a pillow. I don't have a bed. I don't know what you're missing about why I couldn't come to court. I don't have a permanent place to sleep.'"

Public Defender Lauren Anderson recalls one day in court, when she was trying to figure out a better way to resolve these cases for her homeless clients, many of whom just don't come to the courthouse.

"And so it started as kind of an idea to go to the Mission, and take a bus there," recounts Anderson, "and just try to pick everybody up and bring them here one day — and Judge Early's like: 'Why don't we go there?'"

"Right," recalls Municipal Court Judge Sean Early. "I came up with the idea. Might be easier if we just came down to the Mission and brought the court down there."

The first time Judge Early brought his staff, along with city attorneys, to the New Orleans Mission, it was such a success that the second time he convinced Judge Jones, from traffic court, to come, too.

Inside the Mission's main building, Public Defender Laura Bixby stands outside the chapel, waiting to ask people if they want to see one of the judges about a case. It involves some logistics.

"So we can't access court database outside of the court building," explains Bixby. "So we have a couple people at the court, and we basically are like, texting and calling names, and then he's running it on the database, then reporting back to us, like, emailing, faxing, whatever it takes to get some information about the case back over here. So, it's not the most efficient, but…"

But worth it. The idea is to clear warrants for arrest, called attachments, so that people don't get arrested the next time they interact with the police. But a lot of cases get left open simply because they never get updated into the system.

It sounds like people are not even sure what their legal status is a lot of the time.

"Sometimes people know that they missed court," says Bixby. "But a lot of times, you know, people have court cases in four different courts over the span of several different years, and they have no clue which ones they resolved, which ones they missed court on, what happened with the case, what they were even charged with."

"Sometimes it's the fear of you not knowing the outcome and nobody wants negativity or wants to hear no or rejection," says Stanley Walsh, sitting inside what's usually the living room of the Mission's Transitional house, waiting to see a judge. "This is a more friendlier setting. Not police or anything. You know, sometimes people have a fear of the law unnecessarily."

Not so at Municipal Court at the Mission. Here, says Walsh, "you know that they generally trying to help you in this situation. So you're more willing to just come to rectify your problems."

Walsh's friend Tonyell agrees. "Once you come here you're not in a position where you don't know if you're going to walk out. You see what I mean?" asks Tonyell. "So, it's one of those things. You come to a neutral ground outside of the courthouse and you have a possibility of actually leaving."

This fear of court is common, but people are almost never taken into custody simply for showing up. In fact, Desiree Charbonnet, the

chief judge of Municipal Court, says when cases don't involve guns or violence, she does anything she can to not lock up a defendant.

"I'm always looking for ways to divert non-violent offenders from the criminal justice system because I just —over the years I've not seen that having any kind of a positive effect on crime or on their lives, either."

"For every dollar you spend on mental health and substance abuse treatment, you have downstream savings of up to $3 in the criminal justice system," says Jeffrey C. Rouse, a forensic psychiatrist and the Orleans Parish Coroner. In Louisiana, coroners are in charge where the mental health and legal systems intersect.

Nationally, it's estimated that about one-third of chronically homeless people have untreated mental illness. Rouse says once someone's wrapped up in the system, it's a little too late. You can bring them treatment, but the real savings of lives and money is in primary prevention.

"The bottom line is that New Orleans can be a very, very tough place to grow a brain," he says. "From difficulty accessing economic equality; to access to good, nutritious food; to access to good education; to lead poisoning, to early exposure to trauma."

These kinds of systemic problems aren't fixed by arresting people and locking them up — but the court can help. Take David Young. He had a complicated case involving a domestic abuse charge, and at one point, he was suicidal. But through the court he was sent to a mental health facility, and then a drug class. Young was eager to come to the Mission to see his public defender, and the judge.

"He shook my hand, he remembered who I was," recounts Young, beaming. "When I walked in I said 'Thank you again for saving my life.' He did, Judge Early saved my life. He showed concern and just wanting to see me live instead of die."

Then Judge Early did what he'd done for many at Municipal Court at the Mission: he told David Young his fines were dismissed, he had no court costs, and his one year of unsupervised probation was complete.

"There's nothing on my back now," says a relieved Young. "Now I don't have anything to be concerned about as for court, and that really feels good."

Which is exactly the point: to get people out of the system and help them move forward with their lives.

The Link Between Homelessness and Criminal Involvement Isn't Black and White

The Justice Management Institute

The Justice Management Institute is a non-profit organization based in Virginia that contributes education, research, and training in the area of justice policy.

During the holidays, we often reflect on those in our community without housing and suffering from mental illness or other disabling conditions. We wanted to use this opportunity to highlight the challenges that the justice system faces in dealing with the chronically homeless; the actions being taken in Portland, Oregon to address these challenges; and a number of resources that offer guidance for justice practitioners.

[Research] suggests a strong connection between chronic homelessness and criminal justice involvement.

As a society, we have made some progress in the past decade to reduce the national number of chronically homeless individuals, yet the numbers still remain high. The U.S. Department of Housing and Urban Development (HUD) 2013 Annual Homeless Assessment Report to Congressindicates that since 2012, the population of chronically homeless individuals in the United States has declined by more than 7,000, or 7%, to approximately 92,000 individuals in 2013. Among this population of chronically homeless, more than two-thirds of individuals were considered unsheltered at the time of the study. It is important to note that these estimates do not include chronically homeless individuals in families.

Portland, Oregon was identified by the 2013 HUD report as being among the top ten major cities with large chronically homeless populations. The impact on the justice system in Portland, as in other cities and counties across the country, is

"Homelessness and contact with the police," The Justice Management Institute. Reprinted by permission.

notable—frequent contact with police, often resulting in arrest, booking and custody in jail, charges filed, court hearings and, frequently, warrants resulting from failure-to-appear in court. A study conducted by Portland Police Bureau highlights the broader implications of chronic homelessness on the justice system, noting that while individuals with mental illness are not predisposed to violence, homelessness and substance abuse can exacerbate mental health issues and, ultimately, increase the likelihood of contact with law enforcement. Indeed, a monograph produced by Rutgers University Center for Behavioral Health Services and Criminal Justice Research suggests a strong connection between chronic homelessness and criminal justice involvement. Further, the monograph makes the case that homelessness can be considered a factor contributing to increased criminogenic risk resulting from the individual's decreased family support, increased proximity to crime, criminal culture and victimization.

The criminal justice response to chronic homelessness is an example of the expanding and widely varied roles law enforcement is expected to perform in our communities. Portland's experience provides a compelling example that law enforcement officers require new skillsets, including Crisis Intervention Training (CIT) and engagement techniques that build trust and legitimacy with homeless populations, to be effective in this expanding mission. Indeed, Portland's approach incorporates several themes for improving the criminal justice response to chronically homeless and mentally ill individuals discussed in the Rutgers monograph. In particular, Portland's approach seeks to closely integrate and coordinate services toward a holistic, person-centered, approach to the chronically homeless, while recognizing that the response to the individual needs to be flexible and tailored to their specific needs. In addition to implementing a bureau-wide CIT training for officers, Portland recently created a Behavioral Health Unit which combines CIT trained officers with mental health professionals and its Service Coordination Team. Further, Portland has improved the

way it tracks data related to interactions with individuals in crisis and dedicated analyst staff to monitor and report performance.

The Center for Problem Oriented Policing (POP) is a helpful resource for communities that are working to address many of the challenges associated with chronic homelessness as well as providing examples from communities that are having success in improving the ability of law enforcement to respond effectively to chronically homeless individuals and to break the cycle of chronic homelessness. POP identifies several strategies to guide communities in developing responses to the chronically homeless that include increasing public awareness of the underlying issues associated with chronic homelessness, changing law enforcement culture and attitudes toward homelessness and collaboration with service providers, and providing alternatives to homeless encampments. Specifically, POP identifies a strategy of 'housing first' to get the chronically homeless into housing and then engage them in mental health and addictions services.

Housing first is a widely known approach to providing alternatives to emergency and shelter care by providing housing and services to chronic users of these traditional systems. Housing First-type programs first emerged in the 1990s in New York and Toronto and have since been implemented in many communities in the United States and internationally. Unlike some traditional strategies to address chronic utilizers of emergency services, jails, and shelters, Housing First programs typically do not require participants to be sober before entering into housing. However, program participants are paired with a case manager and an interdisciplinary Assertive Community Treatment (ACT) team. A substantial volume of research and evaluation relating to Housing First is available from HUD's Office of Policy Development and Research and the Pathways to Housing research library. New research on Housing First suggests that the strategy can produce significant public health and safety outcomes while saving taxpayers money. These savings include substantial reductions in the use of hospital emergency rooms, jails, and police.

The recent web documentary, Here At Home, produced by the Canadian National Film Board, presents the findings from a study released by the Mental Health Commission of Canada on the impacts and outcomes of the Housing First model. The study was the largest of its kind to implement a randomized controlled trial of Canada's national Housing First strategy and included a total of 2,235 individuals, 1,265 of which were selected for the Housing First program. Researchers tracked service utilization and related costs for these study groups, finding that for the top 10% of study participants (defined as the high service user group), Housing First helped to avoid over $26,000 in costs per individual. In other terms, for every dollar spent on these chronic users, Canadians saved $1.50, reinforcing the strategy of prioritizing housing for individuals who are high utilizers of hospital emergency rooms, social services, and jails. Jail costs alone were reduced by over 35% for the high use group in the Canadian study while the largest aggregate cost reduction occurred in hospital emergency room utilization. Further, the perceptions of safety among program participants increased dramatically due to reductions in use of emergency shelter care and interactions with police and security guards.

Video diaries and interviews presented in the documentary provide additional insight into the challenges and successes of the program participants, including some truly impactful testimonials from the program participants, service providers, and property managers. Combined with the statistical findings from the study, the Here At Home documentary makes a unique and compelling case that addressing chronic homelessness with housing and services can improve public safety and health outcomes. Additionally, Portland's experience demonstrates that providing officers with additional training in Crisis Intervention techniques and building collaboration with service providers can help to ensure we are using our criminal justice dollars to their best effect to mitigate the impacts of chronic homelessness to local justice systems.

CHAPTER 3

Do We Have a Responsibility to Help the Homeless?

Overview: Health, Safety, and Education Are Crucial to a Successful Society

Paul Boden

Paul Boden is the organizing director at the Western Regional Advocacy Project (WRAP), which was created to expose and eliminate the root causes of civil and human rights abuses of people experiencing poverty and homelessness.

M ost people would agree that the Federal government has abandoned any pretense of its responsibility to "ensure safe, decent and affordable" (Housing Act, 1937) housing for the poorest people in our country as it committed to do in 1937 when what is now HUD was formed. After years of funding cuts, neglect and demolitions, the 1998 Congress went so far as to say "the federal government can not be held accountable to ensure housing for even a majority of its citizens" (Quality Housing and Work Responsibility Act, 1998). While they may have ignored their legislative mandate from 1937, they have with great conviction, adhered to the 1998 (lack of) responsibility.

Year after year we hear of yet another series of funding cuts, of Section 8 units being converted to market rate, of additional Public Housing units being demolished with no intention of ever replacing them, and of yet even more tightening of eligibility criteria so as to exclude people from even being able to apply for housing assistance.

Couple this with the loss of factory jobs through corporate tax credits for relocation overseas, ever shrinking time limits on welfare assistance, foreclosures, the rising cost of healthcare and the increasing disparity between rich and poor, absolutely, no wonder that homelessness has stayed with us for the past 30 years. In fact, it would be a miracle if it hadn't.

"Why We Still Have a Massive Homelessness Problem (Hard Times USA)," by Paul Boden, AlterNet, April 17, 2013. Reprinted by permission.

Since 1983, local governments have been expected to manage this crisis with nothing more from the Feds than a miniscule amount of funding for emergency shelters, social workers, and a very small number of transitional housing units. In true Washington DC fashion, local communities are being faced with more and more reporting requirements, more and more information systems programs to comply with, and of course the ever evolving plans they are required to write with the concurrent, and completely useless, oversight commissions they are required to create.

The federal government has effectively transferred responsibility for nationwide, multifaceted, broad-based systemic poverty and homelessness directly onto the backs of local governments and local communities. And for the past 15 years, those local communities have been fighting back with a vengeance. Rather than fight the feds however, they are putting their energies into attacking poor and homeless people. Unfortunately like the kids who get bullied at school and then bully the kids smaller than them, the fighting that is happening isn't coming close to addressing what has everyone so freaked out in the first place – poor and homeless people being forced to live on the street.

The Feds deprive the state and local governments, the state deprives the county and city governments, and in a sure sign of exasperation after years of abuse and neglect, all of them turn around and attack the poor and homeless people who are trying to live out their lives in spite of having no roof over their head.

We have been here before as a country (see Depression). It is a darker side of ourselves we prefer to keep hidden in the crevices where our fears reside. We wish it weren't true or are ashamed of what we are doing, so we pretend it's not really happening. "Anti-Okie would never happen today" or "Sun Down Towns are a relic of our past" we tell ourselves, and maybe even think it might be true. But, deep down, we know it's not.

With sleeping, sitting, and standing again being criminal offenses, California has officially revived an ugly part of its history. We are again using our "criminal justice" systems coupled with

the power of our governmental institutions and media networks in order to demonize, dehumanize, and ultimately criminalize the people who represent to us a reality we don't want to see or face.

If the United States Government doesn't care about "these" people then why the hell should Menifee, California or Santa Cruz or LA? If we can't get (or even expect to receive) the funding restored that would have allowed us to not have the deepening crisis of homelessness that has been evolving since 1983, well then we give up! Quick call the cops, strictly enforce sitting on the sidewalk laws, loitering laws, being in the parks laws, sleeping in a vehicle laws, anti food distribution laws, and of course the tried and true panhandling laws. If we make it so *they*can't sit, sleep, stand still, or ask for alms -- then maybe, we try to convince ourselves, they will leave. And if they don't leave, well we always have that brand new jail we were able to get federal funding to help us build.

It is well past time for us to unite our local governments and our local communities. Fighting with each other over whether life sustaining acts such as sleeping, resting, or eating, are or are not crimes is never ever going to generate the focus and attention on what matters. We need to speak to our federal government with one voice. We need to say that when millions of people are sleeping in our streets and shelters every year and when over 1 million children who go to our public schools everyday don't have a home to go to that night, it is a national crisis that demands a federal response. When we are so clearly able to document the cause and effect of federal housing assistance cuts in the early 1980's with the advent of mass contemporary homeless across the country, it is a national crisis that demands a federal response.

California's Homeless Person's Bill of Rights and Fairness Act (AB 5) authored by assemblymember Tom Ammiano is an attempt to get the State of California to differentiate between criminal acts that a person might commit (regardless of their housing status) and life sustaining acts we all perform but become criminal offenses when those without housing commit them. Oregon, Vermont, Connecticut and Missouri are joining California in calling for a

Homeless Bill of Rights. This signifies a growing dissatisfaction with the current tools and strategies available to localities to address our growing economic disparities that result in human rights abuses.

AB 5 is a bill that says to local governments that regardless of whether or not you are frustrated and angry that the federal government has abandoned your needs, it is not ok for you to take that anger out on people who are less powerful than you. The bullied child need not become the teenage bully.

If we truly embrace its principles, AB 5 is a bill that can unite us all and get us working together for a government that affirms that a healthy, housed and educated people is a righteous responsibility for governments to undertake.

The Government Has a Responsibility to Help the Homeless

Department for Communities and Local Government

This United Kingdom government organization is responsible for constructing places to live and work, and giving more power to its citizens to craft their surroundings.

Ministerial Working Group foreword

This plan is owned by the Ministerial Working Group on Homelessness.

To prevent homelessness and support those without a stable home, a range of Government Departments must work together. Homelessness is more than about housing. For many years there was criticism that policies of different Departments needed to join up. We have come together through the Ministerial Working Group to better prevent and tackle homelessness, and address the underlying causes.

The Government has already shown its commitment to protecting the most vulnerable. It has maintained funding for local authority homelessness services through the Spending Review and recognised the importance of preventing homelessness in the Mental Health and Drugs Strategies, and offender sentencing and rehabilitation green paper.

The Government is committed to addressing the underlying causes of homelessness and social disadvantage by tackling issues of poverty, equality and social justice.

The tough fiscal climate means that it is even more important that we effectively prevent and tackle homelessness. We should be making the most of our investment in services, preventing people from falling into a cycle of repeat homelessness and avoiding increasing costs in the long-run.

"Vision to End Rough Sleeping: No Second Night Out Nationwide," Licensed under Open Government License v3.0/Crown Copyright, July 2011.

This plan sets out six joint commitments that means we will all work together to give local people the tools to tackle rough sleeping and put an end to second nights out on the street. It is the fi report from the Ministerial Working Group as we work to tackle homelessness more effectively, across government.

[...]

Introduction

"For most people, it's not just a single issue. It's not just drugs and alcohol. They have a mental health problem or experience a family crisis. This leads them into drugs and alcohol, which makes it worse." (Homeless Link Advisory Panel member)

Tackling homelessness is at the centre of the Coalition Government's commitment to protect the most vulnerable and promote social justice. As the Prime Minister has made clear, protecting the most vulnerable is "the sign of a civilized society".[1] People living on the streets are some of the most disadvantaged people in society – at risk of severe illness, violence and early death. No one should have to sleep out on our streets in the 21st century.

The Government is committed to preventing and tackling homelessness. We have maintained the level of Preventing Homelessness Grant, with £400m being made available to local authorities and the voluntary sector over the next four years. We have also set out proposed changes in the Localism Bill to give greater freedoms and flexibilities to local authorities to meet the housing needs of homeless families, reducing the need for long waits in temporary accommodation.

The Government recognises that homelessness is about more than just providing housing. Homeless people often have complex underlying problems that can be worsened by living on the streets or in insecure accommodation. The Government has set up a

Ministerial Working Group to bring together eight departments with responsibility for the issues that affect homeless people.

The focus of this plan is on single homeless people who are not in 'priority need',[2] including those who are living on the streets and those who are at the greatest risk of rough sleeping because they have lived on the streets or are living in insecure accommodation, such as hostels or shelters. Rough sleeping is the most visible form of homelessness and where people are the most vulnerable. In London, 52 per cent of rough sleepers have alcohol support needs, 32 per cent drug support needs, and 39 per cent mental health problems. Many have had extensive contact with the state: 37 per cent had previously been in prison, 12 per cent in care and 3 per cent in the UK Armed Forces.[3] These factors can often be linked to social disadvantage. For example, family breakdown, debt and a lack of skills or qualifications. Many have experienced some form of trauma in their life.

The plan sets out six priority areas where government departments and partners have committed to work together to end rough sleeping. The Government fully supports the Mayor's commitment to end rough sleeping in London by 2012. Anyone who finds themselves sleeping rough should be quickly helped off the streets so they do not have to spend a second night without a roof. And to keep people off the streets, services must address the problems that led to homelessness in the first place.

The Ministerial Working Group on Homelessness is helping to ensure that the government works better together. But the most successful action to tackle homelessness is rooted in local communities. Real progress can be made when local authorities work with voluntary and community groups, and with private sector support – a real example of Big Society in action. Local communities will be able to act even more effectively if they are freed from unnecessary bureaucracy.

The economic case for action is as strong as the moral one. Single homeless people are five times more likely to use Accident and Emergency departments than the general public.[4] There

are also negative impacts on communities and industries such as tourism from visible rough sleeping and associated activities, such as begging and street drinking. Despite the tough fi climate and the need to tackle the nation's deficit, we need to 'invest to save' in services which prevent and tackle homelessness. This will reduce the need for more expensive help to address entrenched problems in the future, and avoid passing the costs to other areas or public services.

The new rough sleeping statistics published on 17 February 2011 show that an estimated 1,768 people are sleeping rough in England on any one night.

Previously only local authorities where there was a known, or suspected, rough sleeping problem were required to provide a count. This meant that only 440 rough sleepers were counted under the previous system. Now all areas across England provide counts or robust estimates giving a clear national picture. By having more accurate data in each area, we can better identify rough sleepers and target service provision and action to address the problem.

In addition to people sleeping rough on any one night, a greater number of people will be living in insecure accommodation, such as hostels for short periods of time or staying with friends and family. The lack of a stable home increases the risk that they could be forced to sleep rough at some point. It is important that we continue to tackle the broader isssues of access to stable housing in order to prevent homelessness and avoid long-term impacts. This is the first report from the Ministerial Working Group to meet its aim of ensuring a cross-government approach to preventing and tackling homelessness, and supporting those without a stable home.

This plan is not just for housing providers, but for everyone involved in delivering services that help tackle homelessness, and for everyone who wants to get involved in their local community to help end rough sleeping.

The work of the Ministerial Working Group is specific to England and many of the areas covered in this plan are matters for the devolved administrations in Scotland, Wales and Northern

Ireland. The Scottish Government, Welsh Government and Northern Ireland Executive have their own approaches to tackling homelessness and rough sleeping. Some areas of the plan, such as defence, and social security in Scotland and Wales are non-devolved, though they can interface with a range of devolved matters. A commitment to preventing homelessness is common to all four nations in the United Kingdom. We are therefore committed to working with the devolved administrations on our vision for tackling homelessness.

No Second Night Out nationwide

"If people have no issues, they have no priority status. If someone has drugs or alcohol problems they get priority. But if you leave someone with no issues on the streets, they become more vulnerable to what's out there." (Homeless People's Commissioner)

It cannot be right in the 21st century that anyone should need to sleep on the streets. The Ministerial Working Group has identified that its priority is to ensure that when people hit crisis point and come onto the streets, there is a swift and effective response from services.

Despite the best efforts of local authorities and service providers to prevent homelessness, some people will continue to experience personal crises, which results in them coming onto the streets. People are often drawn to specific locations, such as city centres or seaside resorts, which puts particular pressure on services in these areas. Our aim is to ensure that anyone who does spend a night sleeping rough anywhere in the country is immediately helped off the streets.

London faces particular challenges with 23 per cent of rough sleepers being counted in the capital. The Mayor of London has already devised and launched No Second Night Out. This is

overseen by the Mayor's multi-agency Delivery Board and funded by the Government's Preventing Homelessness Grant.

There is a 24-hour helpline and a website so that members of the public, the emergency services and homeless people themselves can report and refer rough sleepers, with an outreach worker dispatched to contact the person as quickly as possible. An assessment hub, staffed by a professional team, has been set up to provide existing outreach teams with somewhere to take new rough sleepers where they can be assessed and while alternative housing or reconnection back to their home area or country is arranged. Outcomes are tracked using London's rough sleeper database. This approach is being piloted until the end of September 2011 and adjustments to practice will be made as necessary.

The Government recognises that many cities already have excellent homelessness services in place, and have been highly successful at reducing levels of rough sleeping. Local areas have different outreach and other service models, reflecting local circumstances. Local authorities will need to build on these to adopt a gold standard approach to rough sleeping services that meet the No Second Night Out principles:

- New rough sleepers should be identified and helped off the streets immediately so that they do not fall into a dangerous rough sleeping lifestyle
- Members of the public should be able to play an active role by reporting and referring people sleeping rough
- Rough sleepers should be helped to access a place of safety where their needs can be quickly assessed and they can receive advice on their options
- They should be able to access emergency accommodation and other services, such as healthcare, if needed
- If people have come from another area or country and find themselves sleeping rough, the aim should be to reconnect them back to their local community unless there is a good reason why they cannot return. There, they will be able to

access housing and recovery services, and have support from family and friends.

No Second Night Out helps to identify where rough sleepers are coming from and improve prevention and recovery services in these areas. It needs to sit alongside efforts to tackle the multiple needs of the most entrenched rough sleepers through personalised approaches. In London, over three-quarters of the '205' most entrenched rough sleepers targeted by the Mayor's London Delivery Board for extra focus and assistance in May 2009 are no longer sleeping rough.

Robust multi-agency approaches can help people off the streets if they are used alongside offers of appropriate accommodation and support, such as by Newcastle City Council and the Cyrenians as part of the Adults with Chronic Exclusion pilot to help entrenched rough sleepers in Newcastle.[5]

A key success in parts of London, the South-East and Peterborough has been the UK Border Agency's involvement in supporting local authorities' work with migrant rough sleepers. A pilot has carried out 66 administrative removals up until the end of December 2010 where a voluntary return has been refused, with 290 individuals taking up voluntary reconnection offers.

Enforcement provides a solution of last resort, and also often encourages recent migrants to accept an offer of voluntary reconnection which they may have otherwise refused. We will work with voluntary homelessness organisations to help migrants access short-term accommodation where possible while they are seeking work or awaiting reconnection, to prevent rough sleeping on the streets.

The Scottish Government, Welsh Government and Northern Ireland Executive have varying strategies for tackling homelessness and rough sleeping based on historically different approaches. These are based on the understanding that local services developed in response to local circumstances and contexts are more effective in tackling homelessness. One of the key objectives of No Second Night Out, preventing homelessness at the earliest opportunity,

is shared by approaches pursued in all countries. The Devolved Administrations remain committed to implementing policies which will prevent homelessness and tackle rough sleeping through learning and sharing practice with partners across the United Kingdom.

Preventing homelessness

"If you're accessing drug and alcohol treatment, or in the criminal justice system, they should be geared up to be aware of other things that can help to prevent your homelessness. Then you could get help before you lost your fl (Homeless Link Advisory Panel member)

The Government recognises that rough sleeping can be avoided in many cases if people have access to stable accommodation and get help at an earlier stage. It is common sense that we should be preventing homelessness and keeping people off the streets in the first place.

Local authorities already have a duty to ensure that homeless applicants who are not in 'priority need' (and who are eligible for assistance and unintentionally homeless) are provided with advice and assistance to help them secure their own accommodation. Local authorities are also encouraged to prevent homelessness wherever possible. To help them, the Government is maintaining investment in Preventing Homelessness Grant, with £400m over the next four years. Homeless Link will support local authorities to identify opportunities and commission services that better prevent rough sleeping by rolling out the PrOMPT toolkit.[6]

The Government has prioritised help for single homeless people, recognising that they often do not benefit from homelessness prevention schemes. We are providing £10m to Crisis between 2010-11 and 2012-13 to fund voluntary sector schemes to improve access to the private rented sector for single homeless people.

More broadly, the Government has made prevention a central element of a number of cross-government strategies, which recognise the importance of stable accommodation. We have included action on the issues that lead to homelessness in:

- the new Mental Health Strategy[7] which focuses on promoting good mental health and early intervention
- the Drugs Strategy[8] which sets out an ambition for anyone dependent on drugs or alcohol to achieve recovery
- the offender sentencing and rehabilitation green paper[9] which focuses on more effective sentencing and rehabilitation to break the cycle of crime and re-offending
- reforms to the NHS[10] and public health delivery[11] which introduce a prominent role for the NHS and local authorities in tackling health inequalities.

The Ministerial Working Group has focused on providing appropriate support where 'transitions' between different forms of accommodation create the risk of homelessness:

- All offenders at risk of homelessness are identified on arrival into prison. We will publish in 2011 more comprehensive expectations and guidance for Prisons and for Probation Trusts on how to assist offenders to access stable housing
- We will highlight the findings and recommendations from research by Homeless Link to encourage closer working between criminal justice agencies and homelessness organisations[12]
- The National Inclusion Health Board13 will work with the NHS, local government and others to identify what more must be done to prevent people at risk of rough sleeping being discharged from hospital without accommodation
- We will introduce a new approach to the provision of accommodation which better meets the needs of Service personnel during and after Service. We will also enhance the resettlement support to Early Service Leavers. For those veterans experiencing homelessness many years

after discharge, we will work with voluntary homelessness organisations, the new Veterans' Information Service[14] and the Service Personnel and Veterans Agency[15] to promote the through-life support available to former members of the Armed Forces

- We will promote work to prevent and tackle youth homelessness and support care leavers, so that they do not become tomorrow's rough sleepers. We have published statutory guidance for local authorities on homeless 16 and 17 year olds[16] and care leavers[17] which highlights the importance of providing housing with support (and not, for example, Bed and Breakfast accommodation)
- We will work with voluntary homelessness organisations to ensure that migrants from the EU Accession States are prepared before they travel to the UK. We will highlight Jobcentre Plus self-help job-search points and other services where relevant to migrants at risk of rough sleeping.

Improving support services

"You need support coming off the streets. A lot of people get institutionalised while on the streets. When I came off the streets, I needed resettling into a lifestyle that was normal for me. I was still drinking a lot but nobody picked it up. There was no help for drinking or mental health." (Homeless People's Commissioner)

People who have experienced homelessness often need access to specialist services that provide an intensive package of recovery support and address their multiple needs. This requires all relevant organisations to be involved, and the needs of homeless people to be recognised in strategies such as the local Joint Health and Wellbeing Strategy so that relevant services are commissioned.

The involvement of service users helps to improve planning and build the confidence of the people involved.

Some of the most effective delivery models bring services to the homeless person, such as, 'in-reach' into hostels. These services work because they are tailored to address personal needs, for example, through the use of personal budgets or the provision of peer support and mentoring from people who have experienced homelessness. They often offer a pathway approach with a single key worker to provide supported access to services. The voluntary and community sector has an excellent track record of delivering innovative solutions, working alongside statutory services.

The complicated nature of homeless people's needs (such as alcohol or substance misuse together with mental health problems[18]), plus difficulties caused by living in insecure accommodation, means that homeless people often struggle to access the healthcare they need and rely on acute hospital services. The Government will introduce new duties on the NHS Commissioning Board and GP Commissioning Consortia to reduce inequalities in access to, and outcomes from, healthcare.[19] Local authorities will have a new ring-fenced public health budget with a 'health premium' to promote action to reduce health inequalities. Directors of Public Health will be the strategic leaders for public health and health inequalities in local communities. Health and Wellbeing Boards will play a key role in bringing together the NHS, public health and social care services within a local authority area, and developing health and wellbeing strategies based on the Joint Strategic Needs Assessment.

The Government recognises the importance of the Integrated Offender Management approach to join up local action to identify, target and support the most chaotic and problematic offenders, some of whom may be without suitable and sustainable accommodation and at risk of rough sleeping. By joining up at the local level, criminal justice agencies can work with local authorities and others outside the traditional community safety network, such as voluntary sector homelessness organisations, to provide the necessary support to help break the cycle of re-offending and the

factors that drive it, such as homelessness. Government is also supporting the local development of custody suite liaison and court diversion schemes. This will help facilitate closer working between health professionals and criminal justice agencies to ensure that offenders who are homeless or at risk of rough sleeping are able to access treatment services (particularly substance misuse and mental health services).

Homeless people very often want to work – 80 per cent of clients helped by St Mungo's homeless charity said that work was one of their goals.[20] Given the opportunity and the right support, many homeless people – including those experiencing multiple disadvantages – can and do work. Employment represents one of the most sustainable routes out of homelessness and priority should be given to work-related activities at the earliest possible stage of engagement. The introduction of Universal Credit[21] will ensure that work always pays, making it worthwhile for homeless people to undertake work for limited hours in line with their capabilities. Where people are not ready for work, they will be able to instead undertake agreed training or voluntary work aimed at improving their employability, with continued support from the benefits system.

Social enterprise offers a growing and important opportunity that can increase the involvement of people in work. Indeed, the homelessness sector pioneered this approach through The Big Issue. Such innovative approaches show how enterprise can get involved and the success that can result from unlocking the potential of homeless people. Many business, trusts and foundations provide invaluable experience and resources to homelessness organisations. Government will explore the potential of a Social Impact Bond to encourage private and charitable investment in developing innovative services that address the multiple needs of rough sleepers.

People also need a range of accommodation options to suit their needs and support their recovery. Significant progress has been made in transforming the hostel sector to improve standards, raise

aspirations and provide more opportunities for training and work. Government will provide a further £37.5m between 2012-13 and 2014-15 through the Homelessness Change Programme. Some people may be able to move directly into rented accommodation, including those moving-on from hostels, often with support so that the person can manage a tenancy and continue their recovery.

Supported lodgings and foyer schemes play a key role in offering supported accommodation tailored to young people's needs. Women's refuges and hostels for women and couples without children also provide an important source of accommodation, including for people escaping domestic violence. The National Housing Federation is working with its members to examine the role housing associations have in meeting the housing and support needs of vulnerable groups, including single homeless people, and how this can be developed in the future. The Federation will publish its report at the end of the year.

Supporting local action to end rough sleeping

"If you have a service tailored to each person, it's about getting the best service for them. It's not people getting told the same thing that won't help them." (Homeless Link Advisory Panel member)

The Government is clear that communities are best placed to respond to local needs and priorities, and should be in the lead on tackling homelessness. Many homeless services originate from community concerns about vulnerable people. Thousands of people volunteer every week in established homeless day centres, hostels and shelters, helping rough sleepers to come off the streets. Local authorities play a vital role in enabling and co-ordinating activities.

Tackling homelessness will be challenging over the next few years as we tackle the nation's deficit. But it is vital that we prioritise the needs of the most vulnerable to prevent damage to individuals

and communities, and avoid higher costs for local services later on. The Government has prioritised homelessness funding through the Spending Review and provided a clear expectation that councils should not be targeting disproportionate spending reductions on vulnerable people, particularly those who are homeless. It has also provided up to nine months transitional protection and £190m of additional funding to help people affected by the changes to Housing Benefit.

Communities are best able to tackle homelessness when they are freed from unnecessary bureaucratic burdens, have the freedom to align funding to local priorities, and have access to transparent information to monitor the effectiveness of local services. Government has consulted on a new Code of Recommended Practice for Local Authorities on Data Transparency, and will shortly set out minimum standards on the data that should be available and accessible to the public. We will work with the local government sector to support the local collection and publication of relevant data on services to vulnerable people on a comparable basis.

Local political accountability is key to driving up the standards of local services in response to community concerns. The Mayor of London has already demonstrated the successes that can be delivered by strong partnership working facilitated by energetic political leadership. We will continue to encourage councils to create a high profile and give clear local political accountability for tackling homelessness, including encouraging any mayors established in our largest cities to take a personal lead in their area.

The key measure of success of the commitments in this report will be the extent of rough sleeping, as measured by the new more accurate methodology introduced by this Government. In addition, the No Second Night Out approach to service delivery will be rolled out across the country. We will continue to use the data available in London to monitor the fl of new rough sleepers and draw on other sources of information, such as research and reports from the voluntary sector. We will use the new outcome frameworks being

developed by Government to measure the impact of prevention and recovery services, and will explore the use of a single definition for single homeless people to better track people in government data collection systems.

Working together to end rough sleeping

This report sets out shared commitments to end rough sleeping. The Government has prioritised tackling homelessness with a new, more coherent national approach.

We have also set out new freedoms to better support local communities, with commitments from local government and voluntary sector partners on the action that they will take. Our aim is to ensure that people receive the help they need as soon as they come onto the streets and that improved, integrated services are able to support them to remain off the streets.

The Ministerial Working Group will oversee departmental progress against the high- level commitments in this document and work with partners to address the practical barriers to tackling homelessness. The Group will publish an annual update on its progress.

Endnotes

1. Speech to the Conservative Party Conference speech, 6 October 2010.
2. Priority need categories as set out in the homelessness legislation.
3. Street to Home 2010-11 bulletin which uses data from the Combined Homelessness and Information Network (CHAIN) on people seen rough sleeping in London.
4. Healthcare for Single Homeless People, Offi of the Chief Analyst, Department of Health, March 2010. www.dhcarenetworks.org.uk/_library/Resources/Housing/Support_materials/Other_reports_and_guidance/Healthcare_for_single_homeless_people.pdf
5. http://www.thecyrenians.org/
6. Prevention Opportunities Mapping and Planning Toolkit (PrOMPT) www.homeless.org.uk/prompt
7. No Health Without Mental Health, 2 February 2011. www.dh.gov.uk/en/Healthcare/Mentalhealth/MentalHealthStrategy/index.htm
8. Drug Strategy 2010, Reducing demand, restricting supply, building recovery: supporting people to live a drug-free life, 8 December 2010. www.homeoffice.gov.uk/publications/alcohol-drugs/drugs/drug-strategy/drug-strategy-2010
9. Breaking the Cycle Effective Punishment, Rehabilitation and Sentencing of Offenders, 7 December 2010. www.justice.gov.uk/consultations/breaking-cycle-071210.htm

The NHS White Paper, Equity and Excellence: Liberating the NHS, 12 July 2010. www. dh.gov.uk/en/Publicationsandstatistics/Publications/PublicationsPolicyAndGuidance/ DH_117353

10. The NHS White Paper, Equity and Excellence: Liberating the NHS, 12 July 2010. www.dh.gov.uk/en/Publicationsandstatistics/Publications/ PublicationsPolicyAndGuidance/DH_117353

11. Healthy lives, healthy people: our strategy for public health in England, 30 November 2010. www.dh.gov.uk/en/Publichealth/Healthyliveshealthypeople/index.htm

12. Homeless Link is conducting a research project to explore how the homelessness and criminal justice sectors can best support offenders and determine the role they can play in reducing offending behaviour. This report will be published in July 2011. www.homeless. org.uk/criminal-justice-project

13. A National Inclusion Health Board, chaired by Professor Steve Field, has been established to drive ahead the Government's Inclusion Health programme which aims to deliver a step-change in health outcomes for the most vulnerable people in society, including the homeless.

14. The Government has announced that a Veterans' Information Service (VIS) will be put in place so that 12 months after a person leaves the Armed Forces, they will be provided information offering the opportunity to access guidance and support on health and wellbeing issues. This is scheduled for rollout in early 2012. www.mod.uk/DefenceInternet/DefenceNews/DefencePolicyAndBusiness/ ImprovedMentalHealthServicesPledgedForArmedForces.htm

15. www.veterans-uk.info/

16. Provision of Accommodation for 16 and 17 year old young people who may be homeless and/or require accommodation, Department for Children, Schools and Families and the Department for Communities and Local Government, April 2010. www. education.gov.uk/publications/standard/publicationDetail/Page1/DCSF-15005-2010

17. Planning transition to adulthood for care leavers, Department for Education, October 2010. www.education.gov.uk/publications/standard/Lookedafterchildren/Page1/DFE-00554-2010

18. See, for example, Department for Communities and Local Government and the National Mental Health Development Unit, Guidance on meeting the psychological and emotional needs of homeless people, 2010. www.nmhdu.org.uk/our-work/improving-mental- health-care-pathways/non-statutory-guidance-on-dealing-with-complex-trauma-/

19. Subject to Parliamentary approval of the Health and Social Care Bill 2011.

20. Just the Job, St Mungo's, published in July 2010. www.mungos.org/documents/4021

The Government Can't Do It Alone

Government of Western Australia

The Government of Western Australia is made up of more than 100 departments and has made strides to help the homeless by creating a State Plan to address homelessness.

Message from the Minister

Western Australia is a prosperous state, however, many of our citizens do not share in the benefits many of us take for granted. Homelessness affects an estimated 13,000 people in our state including men, women, young people and children. The Western Australian Government is committed to responding in new and sustainable ways to give people at risk of, or experiencing homelessness, the opportunity to move beyond the immediate crisis and into long term sustainable housing.

Homelessness is a serious community issue, often caused by complex, interrelated personal, social and economic factors. Family and relationship breakdown, mental illness, domestic violence, drug and alcohol misuse and disability may lead to homelessness. Coupled with a shortage of affordable housing and unemployment, homelessness may become entrenched.

It is important people experiencing homelessness are supported to address the range of issues contributing to their homelessness and this requires an integrated approach.

This State Plan provides a framework for communities to work together to address homelessness. Partnerships between government agencies and community organisations are the most effective way to help people get their lives back on track and regain the dignity that comes with having a place to call home.

The Western Australian Council on Homelessness has been instrumental in developing this plan and the Council will support the development of regional plans throughout the state. I invite

"Opening Doors to Address Homelessness," Department for Child Protection and Family Support.

you to be part of this process, working together to ensure people who are at risk of, or experiencing homelessness will have access to housing and support to establish a home and a place in the community through an integrated homelessness service system.

Introduction

Over the past decade Western Australia has experienced rapid economic growth. However, not all have benefited from the opportunities of a strong economy. Safe and secure shelter and support is vital to human wellbeing, yet in Western Australia on the last census night in 2006, approximately 13,000 people were homeless.

Without access to permanent safe accommodation and support, people at risk of, or experiencing homelessness are more likely to experience poor health, inadequate schooling/education, violence, prolonged unemployment and social isolation. Responding to homelessness is fundamentally linked to housing however, it is also much more than this. It also involves providing support to meet health, employment, social and personal needs.

The Western Australian community services sector, government and specialist homelessness services have been working for many years to support homeless people. It is now timely to reflect on these responses to homelessness, to build on this work and improve the outcomes. The State Plan identifies an important vision to address homelessness and represents a commitment and renewed focus on intervening early to prevent and reduce homelessness in Western Australia.

The State Plan outlines the outcomes and key principles for implementing an improved integrated approach to homelessness and aims to bring all relevant agencies and services to work together to open doors and improve circumstances for people who are at risk of, or experiencing homelessness. It also identifies the action areas to support flexible and responsive services for people when they are homeless and to prevent people from slipping back into homelessness.

The Western Australian Council on Homelessness has been instrumental in developing the vision, outcomes, guiding principles, action areas and commitment outlined in the State Plan. The Council is made up of community services sector and academic representatives with ex-officio members from key State and Commonwealth government departments. The Council supports the National Affordable Housing Agreement (NAHA) and the new National Partnership Agreement on Homelessness (NPAH) focussing on the three key strategies of:

- Early intervention and prevention;
- A better integrated service system; and
- Breaking the cycle of homelessness.

Outcomes

The State Plan builds on the NAHA and NPAH and contributes to the following outcomes;

Early intervention

1. Services intervene early to help sustain housing and prevent homelessness.
2. Homelessness risk factors are assessed and identified early across a broad range of agencies and services.

Better integrated service system

3. 'No wrong door' - any entry point will be the right entry point for people who are homeless to be assessed, receive and/or linked to appropriate assistance.
4. People are proactively connected to mainstream and allied services.
5. Specialist homelessness services, government departments, mainstream services and the broader community services sector are integrated and work together to address homelessness.

Breaking the cycle

6. Specialist homelessness and mainstream services provide an integrated response to homelessness to move people out of crisis into long term sustainable accommodation.

7. People are supported to access and sustain long term housing and to connect and participate in their community so fewer people remain in or re-enter homelessness.

Principles to Guide Action: How Do We Get There?

There are four guiding principles to support service delivery.

People Centred

There is a need to put people first and provide support that is responsive to an individual's changing needs. The concept of wrap around services will be central to bring together a variety of different responses to meet the complexity of needs experienced by the individual homeless person. Using this approach will build a system that is focused on positive outcomes for individuals.

Leadership

Strong leadership at all levels is required to ensure good outcomes for those at risk of, or experiencing homelessness. All stakeholders including government, community, business and individuals have a role to play in responding to homelessness.

The Department for Child Protection is the lead government department responsible for funding specialist homelessness services and is working closely with other government departments, community organisations and mainstream services to bring together effective responses.

Partnership and Integration

The aim of an integrated service system is to build stronger partnerships between different agencies, service sectors and mainstream services to provide a coordinated response to ensure

people are assisted in a consistent and timely way. This involves a 'no wrong doors' approach to assist people at risk of, or experiencing homelessness, to access the appropriate support and referrals regardless of their initial point of contact with the service system.

Flexibility and Innovation

A service system that is continually improving provides responsive, timely, efficient and effective services and removes barriers that keep people in homelessness. It is also important to build a strong evidence base to inform how responsive and flexible service systems make a difference.

To complement good relationships and partnerships, individuals, services and departments involved need to be flexible. This flexibility should encompass and encourage innovation to create a climate of continuous improvement and responsiveness to people's unique needs, including Aboriginal people and those from Culturally and Linguistically Diverse backgrounds.

Action Areas: More Than a House

The following action areas aim to assist people at risk of, or experiencing homelessness, to access and sustain housing, address underlying needs which exclude them from the community and prevent future episodes of homelessness.

It is not just the role of specialist homelessness services to address homelessness. To be successful, a variety of services and sectors have a role to play, including mainstream and allied services, government and community services.

Range of Housing Options

Addressing homelessness requires linkages to a range of housing options and the provision of appropriate support in order to meet the needs of the individual and ensure sustainable outcomes.

Housing providers, including public housing, community housing and the private sector where possible, should intervene early to assist people to maintain their existing housing. In some cases, services will support people to return to, or continue to live,

in the family home, with other family members or friends or as a member of another household.

Employment, Education and Training

It is essential that mainstream services and specialist homelessness services work together to ensure a seamless pathway into employment, education and training. This is aimed at supporting people to move on after homelessness to actively participate in their community and build their own stable economic future.

Health and Wellbeing

Engaging with mainstream health services can improve underlying health related issues that often result in housing arrangements breaking down. Effective early intervention and prevention is reliant on easy access to mainstream services, including hospitals and medical services, drug and alcohol, mental health, and counselling services.

Connection with Community, Family and Friends

A sense of belonging and connection with a community can build both resilience and a support network for individuals and prevent the continuing cycle of homelessness. It is important for services to actively support people to participate in their community and reconnect with family and friends where possible.

Broader Service Developments

The outcomes, guiding principles and action areas outlined in the State Plan will occur alongside a number of other developments that are underway in Western Australia.

Affordable Housing

In 2009, the Western Australian State Government released two strategic housing reports:

- *More Than A Roof and Four Walls* which was produced by the Social Housing Taskforce; and

- *Housing 2020: Future Directions for Affordable Housing* which provided an initial blueprint for a State Affordable Housing Strategy.

Housing 2020 suggested potential directions for system change including public housing reform, promoting growth through sectors such as community housing, increasing land and housing options, and improving support and transition incentives. These broad reform areas are now being explored through the development of a State Affordable Housing Strategy.

The Strategy will detail a range of actions to increase housing options for those on low and moderate incomes. It will also reflect the directions of the NPAH WA Implementation Plan, particularly the need for effective, integrated services to respond to and reduce homelessness.

Specialist Homelessness Services

There are many non government specialist homelessness agencies at the forefront of delivering services to people at risk of, or experiencing homelessness. Some agencies have already commenced reshaping and reforming how they respond to better meet the needs of people accessing their services. This includes developing improved assessment frameworks and integrated responses to maximise outcomes for people.

Mental Health

In March 2010, the Western Australian Mental Health Commission was established with a focus on improving services for people with a mental illness and their families. The establishment of the Commission is a key step in creating a modern effective mental health system that puts people living with mental illness at its centre and has a clear focus on recovery. The new Mental Health Commission will also actively involve mental health consumers and carers in the planning and delivery of mental health services. This focus on mental health will enable the State to have dedicated

and tailored services that will provide the best possible choices available for people with a mental illness.

The Mental Health Commission is seeking feedback on the WA Mental Health Towards 2020: Consultation Paper. This feedback will further inform the development of the strategic vision and policy for mental health and provide a blueprint for mental health priorities and reform in WA over the next decade.

Family Support

Family support services play an important role in improving outcomes for vulnerable families and individuals. There is a range of services available through Local, State and Commonwealth Governments and the community providing intensive family support and counselling, homelessness services, family and domestic violence intervention, services for young people and parenting support.

The Department for Child Protection, in partnership with the community services sector, will facilitate the development of family support hubs - involving service alliances and common entry points - across metropolitan and regional areas. Family support hubs will connect families and individuals at risk or in crisis, to specialised services that work with vulnerable children, individuals and families. The family support hubs aim to provide a common entry point to deliver a holistic and networked approach to children, individuals and families at risk or experiencing a crisis including those who are homeless.

The 'no wrong door' philosophy will be a key element of the family support hubs and the emphasis will be on supporting clients to access the most appropriate service as soon as possible.

Next Steps: Making it Happen

Regional Plans

The diversity of Western Australia and the unique issues across the regions require customised approaches. Regional plans will be developed across Western Australia to implement an integrated

service system responding to homelessness at a local level. The various mainstream and allied services, government departments, community service sector agencies and specialist homelessness services will be invited to contribute to the reform of the system in line with the principles and outcomes set out in the State Plan.

Individual agencies and workers will be encouraged to identify ways their own agencies and work practices can contribute to the reform agenda. Service users will also be invited to contribute their experiences and ideas to the reform agenda. Each region will be encouraged to develop suitable strategies for consumer participation and comment.

The Western Australian Council on Homelessness will be convening regional seminars with senior government officers and local stakeholders to facilitate the development of regional plans.

Funding and Contracting

Specialist homelessness services are currently funded through the NAHA and, commencing in 2010, new funding has been made available through the NPAH. The new NPAH funding complements and builds on the work of existing NAHA specialist homelessness services.

Around 110 new non-government sector homelessness workers around the State will support people with a variety of needs. This includes people who are sleeping rough, people needing assistance to find and maintain accommodation, or assistance to maintain their private tenancy and avoid eviction and possible homelessness. At least 11% of people assisted will be Aboriginal.

Contract arrangements will be streamlined to ensure flexible innovative responses are easily implemented, and services are not overburdened by red tape and onerous reporting requirements. In addition, flexible brokerage funding has been incorporated for new NPAH services to respond better to individual client needs and to facilitate an integrated approach between specialist homelessness services and mainstream agencies.

Governance and Leveraging Change

The Western Australian Council on Homelessness plays an important role and is responsible for providing advice and support on the NPAH initiatives, contributing to the development and implementation of the State and regional plans, and supporting initiatives that prevent, reduce and end homelessness.

Government agencies are involved in the implementation of the NPAH and are working together to improve services and better integrate with specialist homelessness services. The State government departments involved in addressing homelessness include:

- Department for Child Protection;
- Department of Housing;
- Mental Health Commission;
- Drug and Alcohol Office;
- Department of Corrective Services; and • Western Australia Police.

As the lead agency, the Department for Child Protection is working collaboratively with key departments and mainstream services to promote an integrated, seamless response for people at risk of, or experiencing homelessness. For example, the Departments of Housing and Child Protection have worked together to develop processes to ensure that the allocation of properties is linked with support services provided through the NPAH. The WA Police and the Department for Child Protection have also worked side by side with domestic violence services to ensure referral and information processes are shared to maximise the safety of women and children experiencing domestic violence.

Australian Government departments, such as the Department of Families, Housing, Community Services and Indigenous Affairs (FaHCSIA), administer a number of programs for homeless families and young people, and those at risk of homelessness, and work at a national level to reform and improve connections between services. Centrelink aims to ensure people at risk of,

or experiencing homelessness, are identified early and receive timely responses.

The State Government and the community services sector have already begun work to bring about reforms to the response to homelessness. Reform across specialist homelessness services, mainstream and allied services, government and the community services sector offers real opportunities for change and significant improvement to alter the lives of people at risk of, or experiencing homelessness.

Learning and Promoting Best Practice

In Western Australia, there are a number of non government specialist homelessness services and mainstream government services providing innovative responses and achieving outstanding results. It's important that quality services are acknowledged and their work is promoted as best practice examples both as learning opportunities for others and to reward their efforts.

Promoting best practice and sharing learning will be facilitated though program forums to provide an opportunity to develop and share ideas. The forums will also act as a focus for training, professional learning and development for services and staff.

Measuring Success

An evaluation framework has been developed for the WA NPAH to collect data and monitor progress. The Hierarchy of Intended Outcomes in Appendix 1 offers a guide for both monitoring and evaluation. Elements of the evaluation include:

- Quantitative and qualitative data and reports from service providers, including case studies to identify outcomes achieved and how services are making a difference;
- Exit interviews as part of case management; and
- Annual satisfaction surveys to obtain feedback from people who are at risk of, or experiencing homelessness.

Improved data collection and reporting systems are being developed at both Commonwealth and State levels to help better

understand the support provided and outcomes achieved for people at risk of, or experiencing homelessness.

All Western Australian initiatives will be independently evaluated to identify outcomes achieved. Learning from the evaluations will be circulated throughout the sector to improve responses to homelessness and develop further initiatives.

The Wealthy Need to Step Up

Bill & Melinda Gates Foundation

Founded in 2000, the Bill & Melinda Gates Foundation is a private foundation that aims to improve healthcare and reduce poverty around the world.

The Challenge

Washington State is a center of innovation and home to some of the most successful businesses in the world, but problems of social inequity and poverty persist. Too many families with children are homeless. In fact, in a count led by schools in Washington State during the 2011-2012 school year—as required by the McKinney-Vento Act—more than 27,000 students were identified as homeless. Homelessness has a profound impact on children's health and education, as well as parents' abilities to find a job and stay employed. Homeless children have twice the rate of emotional and behavioral issues—including anxiety, depression, and withdrawal.

Families can become homeless for many reasons. Today's still fragile economy means that more families are unemployed, are earning lower wages, or have lost a home to foreclosure. Other factors—such as domestic violence, medical crises, and mental health or addiction—make families vulnerable. Even in the best economic times, affordable housing can be hard to find for families without skilled jobs.

The Opportunity

In 2000, as a first step in addressing family homelessness in Washington State, the foundation launched the Sound Families Initiative, an eight-year, $40 million program aimed at tripling the amount of available transitional housing—and pairing it with support services in the state's three most populous counties: King, Pierce, and Snohomish. By its close in 2008, the initiative had

"Washington State Homelessness and Family Stability," Bill & Melinda Gates Foundation. Reprinted by permission.

spurred the creation of more than 1,400 transitional homes for families emerging from homelessness.

Family homelessness has persisted, however, and the job is far from done. Meaningful reductions in family homelessness can be achieved only through a systematic, coordinated approach that provides at-risk families with the help they need, when they need it. Until recently, families who became homeless in Washington State had to contact multiple agencies for different kinds of assistance. Many languished on waiting lists for months. Those who obtained temporary housing often had to wait more than a year to get into a permanent home.

All of this is slowly beginning to change. In 2009, partners in King, Pierce, and Snohomish counties boldly declared their commitment to dramatically reduce family homelessness. They joined with the private sector, nonprofits, and Washington State to sign a Memorandum of Understanding pledging to redouble efforts to reduce family homelessness over the next decade. With Building Changes—a nonprofit organization with more than 20 years of experience in homelessness—poised to lead the work, the time had come for a comprehensive response to homelessness.

Our Strategy

To cut key indicators of family homelessness in the Puget Sound region in half by 2020, we believe we must change the way that systems work to address the issue. The foundation is investing in a new approach, based on promising practices from around the nation and lessons we have learned from our work locally. We are working with Building Changes and the governments of King, Pierce, and Snohomish counties to more efficiently deploy existing funding and services from a broad range of sources.

By 2020, we will work with these partners to reduce by half: the number of families that experience an episode of homelessness; the length of time families remain homeless; and the number of families returning to homelessness.

In seeking to achieve these specific outcomes, our work seeks to influence a number of other indicators of family and child well-being that affect families in crisis.

To bring about systemic improvements, we identified five principles that have helped successfully reduce family homelessness in other U.S. communities. These principles guide our investments and the work of our community partners:

- Prevention. We can help keep families in their homes and prevent them from becoming homeless with services such as landlord mediation, help with overdue rent and utility bills, and emergency food, clothing, childcare, and transportation assistance.
- Coordinated entry. Having one simple way to access support services—or one place to go for assistance— helps families get the help they need as quickly as possible and reduces waste and redundancies in the system.
- Rapid housing placement. We work to reduce the time families stay in emergency shelters with quick placements into permanent housing, often with rent subsidies tailored to each family's specific situation.
- Tailored programs. Flexible, coordinated support services that are tailored to each family's specific needs are essential to helping them rebuild and maintain stability and self-sufficiency.
- Economic opportunity. Housing stability depends on good-paying jobs and stable, long-term employment. By linking services with income assistance, education, and employment programs, we can help people find jobs and remain in their homes.

By applying these principles, we believe we can make the best use of a broad array of existing resources, promoting both financial efficiencies while maximizing the most effective use of housing and services.

Government Funded Shelter Isn't as Crucial as We Think

Dr. Tracy Miller

Dr. Tracy Miller holds a Ph.D. from University of Chicago and studies and researches economic theory and policy at The Center for Vision & Values.

D uring a recent trip to Chicago, I couldn't help but notice the large number of homeless people in the downtown area, including one homeless man pushing a child in a stroller. Homelessness was frequently discussed during the 1980s, but seems to receive less media attention now. And yet, the number of homeless today is approximately twice as large as it was in the 1980s.

Homelessness, like any other social problem, is influenced by incentives. Unfortunately, government policy may actually be making the problem worse, particularly government-subsidized housing for the poor.

Many cities have constructed homeless shelters to provide a place for the homeless to stay out of the cold. By the late 1980s, governments created a network of shelters and soup kitchens to feed and house between 200,000 and 300,000 people per day. Between 1988 and 1996, some 275,000 permanent and transitional housing units intended for homeless persons were added. By 1996, roughly 607,000 beds were available as part of the homeless service system in the United States.

There is little evidence to suggest that government-provided shelter has in any way solved or even reduced the problem of homelessness—to the contrary, as noted, the total number of homeless has risen. While advocates for the homeless recognize this, many believe that providing other forms of government

"Homelessness: How Government Policy Makes It Worse," by Tracy Miller, The Center for Vision & Values at Grove City College, May 25, 2012. Reprinted by permission.

assistance will help people avoid homelessness or escape it. In their view, helping people get government-funded rental assistance, food stamps, and welfare checks is integral to preventing homelessness. Some contend that supplying the homeless and those at risk of becoming homeless with permanent housing at government expense will get homeless people off the streets so they can live stable lives.

In truth, lack of affordable housing is not the main reason that people become homeless, although it may be a contributing factor in some cities. People sometimes become homeless due to habits or addictions that lead to mismanagement of their finances, unstable family relationships, and the inability to keep a regular job. According to Martha Burt of the Urban Institute, three quarters of those who are homeless report having problems with alcohol, drug abuse, or mental illness.

Oftentimes, providing government-funded services to the homeless with no strings attached only makes it easier for some of them to continue their bad habits, whether the problem is substance abuse or an unwillingness to accept responsibility for personal behavior. This explains why homelessness did not decline but increased between the early 1980s and 2007, even though the economy was booming and unemployment and poverty were declining. Christopher Jencks argues that shelters made homelessness less painful; this meant that the homeless were "less willing to sacrifice their pride, their self-respect or their cocaine fix to avoid" homelessness. For many people, the availability of shelters seems to increase the incentive to become homeless rather than (if possible) choosing to live with a relative or friend.

Not only does the availability of temporary shelters frequently encourage homelessness, but so does federal housing policy. Many single-parent families would like to move into government-subsidized housing. Because it is in short supply, they would have to wait years for a subsidized apartment to open up. By becoming homeless, a family who was living in someone else's home can move to the front of the line for government-subsidized housing.

Likewise, another form of government assistance is problematic: Government programs that try to provide people with skills and treatment to overcome addictions and psychoses are expensive and have low rates of success. The success rate of some private programs to help the homeless is much higher than government programs—as high as 85 percent. While government programs continue to be funded even if they are ineffective, private charitable organizations' long-term survival depends on getting good results. Successful private programs usually continue to attract donors and volunteers, including former homeless people who themselves have been helped.

It is only natural to feel sympathy for the plight of the homeless. The solution to homelessness, however, is not more handouts from government. Homelessness can be prevented or overcome when a caring community helps those at risk to develop self-discipline and a good work ethic. This is not easy to do, but some private organizations are already doing good work in this area. Those organizations might grow and multiply and also be more effective if government programs, which often interfere with private efforts, were scaled back or eliminated.

People from All Walks of Life Can End Up on the Street

Kylyssa Shay

Kylyssa Shay, formerly homeless and living on the streets, is a writer and artist who also lives with high-functioning autism.

What Causes Homelessness? Maybe It Isn't What You Think.

Many people feel that all homeless people are entirely to blame for their own miserable situations. Those same people tend to believe that under no circumstance could *they* find themselves without a home because they feel they are better than *"those people"* who have lost their homes. In reality, people from all walks of life can wind up on the street and almost no one is immune from the possibility.

I want to present a few reasons actual people become homeless, reasons often beyond their control or ability to deal with. By doing so, I hope to increase empathy towards those less fortunate. **This is by no means an exhaustive list; please do not be offended if you know of something not mentioned on this page.**

Most people become homeless due to circumstances that have overwhelmed them combined with the lack of a family support structure. Others, particularly teens, often lose their housing due to an actively hostile, perhaps even hazardous, abusive, or non-supportive family environment.

Average people without a good friend and family support structure can be overwhelmed by events such as domestic abuse, divorce, unemployment, or illness and find themselves without housing as well. There are many causes of homelessness and while this page covers a few there are almost as many causes as there are people with nowhere to live. If you've ever wondered, "Why do people become homeless?" you've found the right place to learn some of the possible answers.

Lack of a Living Wage: Inadequate Wages Cause Homelessness

Many homeless people work. However, the minimum wage is often not up to the task of supporting a family.

In many areas, working full time for minimum wage does not earn enough to pay rent, utilities and food. While people can combine incomes to rent an apartment they often run into snags such as discovering that the number of working adults required to cover rent and bills combined with their minor children will exceed the number of occupants allowed by their lease. Additionally, many apartment complexes run credit checks which can prevent people with poor credit from renting; things like unpaid medical bills can prevent working people from finding a place to rent.

Parental Ideology

When parents' beliefs clash with teens' beliefs, sexual orientation, or behaviors this may result in teen homelessness.

While few will admit it, some parents only love their children conditionally and these parents may discard their children once they reach their teens. These parents hold their beliefs as more important than their own children. Often the beliefs in question are religious.

As many as 40% of homeless teenagers are lgbt (lesbian, gay, bisexual, or transgendered) when it is estimated that less than five percent of teens are gay, bisexual, or transgendered. In my experience with lgbt homeless teens and young adults, they've come from families that refused to accept them or that began to actively abuse them after their orientation became known.

Perhaps it was a coincidence, but almost all of the gay and bisexual teens and young adults without homes that I've met came from religious fundamentalist homes - fundamentalist Christian, Jewish, and Muslim homes - where their parents' beliefs were anathema to homosexuality or difference of any kind.

I also encountered teens living on the street whose problem stemmed from other religious differences. Some teens and young

adults I met suffered homelessness because they were somehow at odds with their parents' beliefs. In one case, the teenager had converted to Christianity from Islam, in another a teen was suspected of engaging in pre-marital sex which was in conflict with her parents' religious beliefs. A number of Pagan teens that I met were expelled from their Christian homes.

Some of these young people were brutally beaten, threatened with death, or thrown from their homes by force. Others were systematically abused - physically and emotionally - until they ran from their abusers, preferring homelessness to continued abuse.

This subject is practically taboo, the relationship between parental beliefs and teen and young adult homelessness. In fact, after including the concept on a couple of pages, I have received threats, death threats, and hate mail. It is true that child abandonment and abuse are counter to what the vast majority of religious people hold dear. But it is also true that a minority of religious people have a different view. While that minority may seem inconsequential it is anything but inconsequential to around 400,000 American teens and young adults each year.

Physical Illness or Injury

Injury or illness can result in job loss and debt or inability to work.

Some people are on the streets due to injury or illness. Many of them had jobs and insurance but through the course of their medical problems, both were lost. Many people don't realize that even "good" medical insurance is not a guarantee of medical care. They are then devastated to find out that their insurance will not cover their medical expenses or treatment. They are also shocked when they lose their health insurance due to illness or injury.

Hospitalization quickly consumes savings and too many absences from work due to injury or illness will result in the loss of a job. Once a person has a significant gap in his or her employment history and a bad credit score due to unpaid bills it becomes much more difficult for him or her to get a job even when completely recovered.

People in all stages of recovery from illness or injury lose their homes. Some never get well due to lack of treatment and are too ill to hold down a job. Others get well but get pulled down by their medical debt and illness or injury related job loss. And increasingly, medical bankruptcy can result in homelessness.

While many people in situations like these have strong friend and family support structures, many do not. They are the ones who fall through the cracks and find themselves living on the street due to illness, injury, or the resultant medical bills.

It is my sincere hope that this reason for homelessness may disappear through effective health care reform. The health care bill that passed is not even close to what is needed. Medical bills are currently the leading cause of bankruptcy in America, and by a very large margin. Surprisingly, over half of those claiming medical bankruptcy either have or had medical insurance at the time their debt was incurred.

Sexual, Physical, and Emotional Abuse

Abuse can directly or indirectly result in the loss of housing.

Many of the homeless women, teens, and young adults I've met became so because they tried to escape an abusive situation. Some may argue that help is available but people in those situations might not have the access to such help or even know that it exists. Once they become lose their homes, those types of help often become completely inaccessible to them.

Women and teens subjected to sexual, emotional, or physical abuse are at particular risk for homelessness. Many of them also do not realize that running away from their abusive situation may just get them out of the frying pan and into the fire, exposing them to other types of abuse by different people while living on the street.

This is a major cause of homelessness, especially among teens and women. Sometimes people find themselves in domestic abuse situations so frightening they can think of nothing but getting away.

Domestic abuse can also cause its victims to be evicted from their apartments in some states wherein landlords are either

allowed or required to evict tenants who have called police to respond to domestic abuse situations.

Developmental Disorders and Mental Illness

Without a sound family support structure, people with developmental disorders or mental illnesses may lose their housing.

Lack of family support is a major issue for people with disorders such as autism or other mental or emotional issues which make interpersonal relationships difficult. Once such people become teens or adults their families will often step away assuming that such problems evaporate or are cured with adulthood, sometimes resulting in homelessness.

With proper treatment some children with autism or other developmental disorders can go on to lead independent and productive lives. But proper treatment can be a rarity, especially in the American health care insurance system which categorizes treatment of psychological and psychiatric disorders as elective.

Many in the American culture also do not recognize the reality or seriousness of mental illness. Mental and emotional disorders are seen as character defects which anyone can get over without outside assistance by using their own willpower. The insurance based health care system encourages this view because if not required to pay for treatment for mental, developmental, and emotional illnesses and disorders insurance companies save millions if not billions of dollars. Some American religious subcultures such as Scientologists, some Christian Fundamentalists fringe groups, and splinter groups from Christianity and other religions also encourage this view to keep mental and emotional well-being under their control. Thankfully, these attitudes seem to be slowly disappearing in most mainstream belief systems.

But developmental disorders and mental illnesses are real and they don't go away magically upon adulthood. Treatment is required for people suffering from developmental disorders and mental illnesses, and even then, not all sufferers are capable of becoming completely independent.

I fell into this category, a young adult with Asperger's, PTSD, and other emotional illnesses - untreated and left on my own without a family support structure to assist me or for me to rely on.

Is Homelessness a Choice?

Many people believe homelessness is always the result of poor choices, that people choose to be mentally ill, to be physically ill or disabled, to lose their jobs, or to become addicted to drugs. I believe that it is rarely a choice. What do you think?

Even the Wealthy Can Become Homeless

Natalia

Natalia is a former homeless woman who was born in Nigeria and has since turned her life around.

I was born in Nigeria, and contrary to the prevalent view of Africa, I had a good life. My father was a high-ranking politician and my mother earned so much running a chicken farm that she out-earned my father.

But, during my childhood, my mother wanted me and my brothers to have better opportunities and a better education. First she sent my oldest brother to America. Then, when I was 10, she moved me and my other brother to England to attend a posh boarding school (non-citizens are not technically allowed to benefit from the free, public education system in England).

My father stayed behind in Nigeria at his job, but paid for the boarding school. My mother joined the two of us a year later, with plans to start her own business, a bed and breakfast. My father sent her money to help with the down payment and mortgage on a nice house in London. She studied for a master's degree in tourism and hospitality to make her dream business a reality.

When Things Started to Go Downhill

In 2001, my brother living in the U.K. left to join my other brother in America and attend college. Now it was just me and my mum, and because I was at boarding school, I was away from home for long stretches of time.

My mother started attending the UCKG church, a controversial international church that tells its members that God wants them to be rich, drive a nice car and live in a nice house–as long as they donate plenty of money to the church. Her degree in tourism

"I Was Homeless: How It Happened, and How I Got Out," by Natalia, LearnVest, Inc., August 13, 2012. Reprinted by permission.

turned out not to be as useful as she hoped, and the only jobs that came her way were menial.

She was a cleaner, a home care assistant, a newspaper deliverer and even started her own home cleaning business. She could never stick to one thing, getting frustrated or "inspired" and moving on to the next, making about £8,000 a year. Because of her relationship with the church, she believed she wasn't at her full potential because Satan was trying to stop her. She made me attend church with her and watch religious programming on TV. I didn't believe in all this at first, but you just can't say no as a Nigerian child. Because no one else was there to challenge her religious views, I gradually came to believe in them, too.

Seeing what was happening in our lives, I was terrified.

My mother became depressed. She spent all day watching televangelists, not leaving the house for weeks at a time. She tithed 10% of whatever she was making. That wasn't bad, but when I saw a check for $1,000 in her checkbook, she told me, "I paid that thousand so I could pay your school fees." She had watched a telethon where they said, "God told us that the next 100 people who call and donate will get their donation back to them 100-fold."

They didn't mention they had recorded the telethon days earlier.

Because of her tithing and low wages, all our money seemed to disappear right away, and our living conditions quickly spiraled downward.

Thank God They Can't Shut Off the Water

In Nigerian culture, the parents talk among themselves and the kids aren't involved in family conversations, so I never got the chance to tell my father what was going on. He wanted to come join us, but he couldn't leave his job or even visit–he kept applying for a visa and was denied. Meanwhile, he was sending the bulk of his money to pay for my brothers' college educations, thinking my mum and I were doing all right.

When I was at home from boarding school during the summer or weekends, I had almost no food to eat. I survived by eating one

meal of baked beans and rice a day. The telephone and TV got cut off, so I went to the library to use the internet. Utility companies can't legally cut off the electricity or water; they can't let people die in their houses, thank God.

Our car broke down, so I took the train to school extra early to prevent anyone from seeing me walking down the road from the train station. I couldn't afford clothing, so I would rummage through the lost property left behind at the gym.

At home, we had debt collectors banging on our door, and my mother's bank account was blocked. To its credit, the school never said a word to me directly about our unpaid school fees, and I kept going to classes, racking up a bill of £15,000 which never got paid.

When I tried to tell my friends about our situation, they would say, "Oh, all right," and wouldn't offer any help. I got angry and wondered, *Why even bother?* So I hid it from everyone.

When school ended, I didn't even have £20 for the train ticket to take the G.C.S.E. exams, which are like the SATs. Finally, my father told me to use my uncle's credit card, which up until this point my mother had refused to use, even to buy a train ticket. I barely made it in time, but somehow I scored all A's and B's.

Finally, my father visited for the first and last time. It was then he saw our living conditions and realized how bad the situation really was. He bought me a laptop in preparation for college. I thought perhaps now he would be able to help us, but he was powerless to convince my mother to hold down a job and stop giving away all our money. She didn't want to move back to Nigeria, either, and never gave me the choice to.

The Beginning of the End

One day when I was cleaning the house, I found shopping bags stuffed full of two years' unpaid bills. The mortgage company had been trying to repossess the house but had been denied twice by the judge because they didn't have the proper paperwork. I tried to convince my mother to move to a smaller home–we had a modest

four-bedroom–closer to school so we could save on the cost of boarding at my school.

But she saw the two court rulings as a sign from God that he wouldn't let our house get taken away.

We had no money for me to go back to school for my final two years, but my G.S.E.C. exams count as SATs and compulsive schooling ends at 16 in the U.K., so in January of 2007, at my family's urging, I applied to a small college called St. Cloud University in Minnesota. I don't think they could have afforded it, but they thought they would trust God and wing it, and since my brother was living near the school, I would be okay. That was pretty typical thinking on my father and mother's part.

In February, the mortgage company wrote a final letter, telling us our eviction date was May 18th. We just prayed. My acceptance email from St. Cloud came, and I made plans to attend college in the fall.

The day of the eviction, they gave us one hour to pack everything up. We took very little, just clothes and my computer, because my mom said, "We'll be back in one week, tops." The eviction company left a note on our door asking us to call them and get our stuff, but eventually they gave up and burned all our possessions. My passport, exam certificates, prom dress, childhood possessions … my entire life, gone.

We were officially homeless, though we hadn't hit bottom yet.

Out on the Streets

When my father found out we lost the house, he sent money for rent … but instead we spent it at cheap hotels. My mother continued to tithe. She thought that the only way to get out of our situation was to send money to religious organizations, and God would help us.

My father got frustrated and stopped sending money for about five or six months. When we ran out of money, I spent my first night on the streets of London. My mum and I wandered around all the tourist places, until we finally fell asleep in a train station. I

sat in a photo-booth and drew the curtain, shivering. My mother called my father and said, "We slept on the streets."

What could he do? He sent money.

The Turning Point

One day, I passed our old house and I went to look at it. When I realized someone was living there, I walked away crying. When I told my mother, she started sobbing. "I wish you hadn't done that. You just messed up my faith."

That was when I finally realized her faith didn't make any sense. And yet I wouldn't fully accept that she had a mental illness for several more years.

We continued to bounce from place to place. Because I was barely getting enough food to eat or the basic necessities, I wasn't sure how long I was going to be on earth anymore, and I wanted to leave a record of this homelessness and what drove me to this point. So I started a blog, posting every month or so using the laptop my father had given me. It wasn't much, but I wrote when I could. I started getting traffic, and I did a couple of anonymous interviews on smaller internet radio stations. I went to great lengths to hide who I was, using different email addresses and hiding my IP address. My friends were reaching out to me via social networks to figure out where I'd disappeared to, but I ignored them.

Meanwhile, we went from hotel to hotel all over southern England, wasting the money my father sent us. When the money ran out, my mother called family friends she hadn't spoken to in years and we would stay with them until they asked us to leave. We did this to four different families. One time, we were supposed to get a wire transfer on a certain day from my dad, but it didn't come through on time. We fell asleep in the market, and while I shivered in the dark, somebody who was drunk and didn't see me peed right next to me.

From there, we moved into a dingy hotel room with one bed. It was 2010 and I was 21.

How I Got Out

It would be the perfect ending to say I got out of homelessness because of my determination. But the truth is I got out because I asked for help. I met a man who was doing repairs for the landlady whose room we were renting. He and I started dating. But eventually he said, "There's something really wrong here. I don't know what it is."

I told him about my homelessness, about my mother's delusions. And he said, "Why don't you come live with me?"

"Why would you want to help me?" I asked.

"Because you need help," he said. I realized then that I could ask for help and receive it. I needed somebody to believe in me, and he did.

Severing Ties With My Mother

I thought by now this whole saga would be over, but the crap kept coming. My mother disapproved of my boyfriend because he was the wrong religion and older than I am. When I moved in with him, she stalked us, peering in his windows. She cared more about my dating the wrong guy than my getting off the street.

Now she's a week away from being homeless. She's known since April that she needs to leave her apartment but refuses to move in with us or even let me find her a new place.

My gut is telling me maybe I should just let her make her own decisions. I know that is cruel, but I can't even convince her to take a free eye test, much less get her to go to the doctor and get medication. In Nigeria, mental illness is something we don't acknowledge or admit exists.

Getting Back on My Feet

Now I'm technically a visa overstayer (something else my mother said God would take care of) and can't work, so temporarily I consider my blog, which I've taken back up regularly, my job. I'm applying to get a visa, but without a passport, it's difficult. I have to prove that I'm more English than Nigerian now.

I feel a bit of an anti-feminist admitting that my dad and my boyfriend support me, but I'm not spending much, and I'm not in any debt. I think that's an amazing accomplishment. I'm petrified of credit cards.

My boyfriend, whom I will have been dating for two years this month, encouraged me to start studying again. I'm self-studying for the exams we call the A-levels, which I will finish in January. Then I'll be able to attend university.

I would like to be a writer. If that doesn't work out, I'm going to try to do something in sociology or science.

I was once homeless, but I am not hopeless.

Would Ending Homelessness Help Reduce Street Crime?

Overview: There's a Two-Way Cycle Between Homelessness and Crime

Sheri Cartwright

Sheri Cartwright runs the Community Dialogue website and is involved in community building and creating awareness in hopes of helping to break down barriers and stereotypes to help create a healthier, safer community.

A couple of years ago I was blessed with the opportunity to volunteer with the vulnerable sector here in Kitchener/Waterloo. Specifically, I volunteered with homeless youth under age 25. During this time I was able to get to know many of the youth and listen to their stories. My very first shift I went home an emotional wreck after having a conversation with a young girl not much older than my own daughter.

It wasn't long before I became acutely aware of the higher incidence of drug use, mental health problems and criminal activity among this population.

Someone said to me one day, 'they have a choice, we all have choices.' My reply was 'sure we all have choices but we have not all been given the same tools to make good choices. How can I compare myself, who grew up with 2 upstanding parents and all the social support a child should need to someone who was sexually abused from the time they could walk or someone who was given their first hit of crack by their own mother at the age of 16.' Unfortunately many of our homeless population were not raised with good role models or a good set of standards. They once left the hospital as precious, innocent and adorable as any other infant. What they went home to however, is more often than not less than acceptable. Fast forward several years and we

"Fighting the Battle against Crime by Reducing Homelessness," Waterloo Region Crime Prevention Council, August 26, 2013. Reprinted by permission

find an adult struggling with addiction, mental health issues and homelessness all leading to criminal activity.

Here we find the beginning of a two-way cycle. Those who are homeless have a higher probability of ending up in prison while those being released from prison have a higher likelihood of ending up homeless. Once someone has a criminal record it is very difficult to find a job no matter how hard they try to change their life around. Often the rejection turns them back to crime. The same goes for substance abuse where substance abuse often leads to homelessness and homelessness often leads to substance abuse. Addictions often cause someone to lose their job and housing. Using drugs or alcohol also becomes a way to cope with life on the street.

On the other side we have a society that is often quick to judge and quick to condemn often due to a lack of awareness. People feel uncomfortable with it and try to look the other way. It's easier to make donations to charities such as to the food bank than to look in the face of a homeless person on the street.

While food banks and shelters do a great job of providing for immediate needs, they are merely band-aid solutions. They treat the immediate problem not the root of the problem. What we need is to create awareness for other fundamental necessities for tackling homelessness and the crime it brings with it.

We need a plan to create awareness of costs of providing stable housing versus the much higher costs of providing services to the homeless. (ie. Institution, shelters, healthcare, and social services) It is difficult for someone without a place to call home to receive and accept the help they need for addiction and mental health. Without this there is difficulty in reducing the crime rate. Those who seek treatment such as rehab often have nowhere else to go but back in the same street or shelter environment, making relapse highly likely. It's a set-up for failure. When we provide those in need with stable housing we give the opportunity to live with dignity, reduce crime, reduce addiction and give the opportunity for better success. It is a win, win situation. The more people we

help get into stable housing the less financial burden on society and less crime in our community. We build a system that encourages social competency. Give respect to gain respect. This is the message we need to get out. We need to put as much effort into creating awareness and fundraising for this as we do when collecting food and socks.

The diagram below shows the connection between homelessness, substance abuse, mental health, crime and unemployment. If we take homelessness out we have a better chance at battling the other problems.

Let's help society to see the person behind the face. Let's take the homeless away from the street environment and give them a place to call home and give them some dignity and a foundation in which to grow.

Santa Ana Sees the Direct Correlation Between Homelessness and Crime

Theresa Walker and Jordan Graham

Theresa Walker and Jordan Graham are staff writers for the Orange County Register, a Santa Ana, CA based news website.

A typical day in the Santa Ana Civic Center is filled with hazard. Open drug use. Assaults and rape. Urine and feces on public walkways. Untreated illnesses. Sex acts in public.

The exploding transient population in the county's seat of government is clashing in increasingly uncomfortable – and harmful – ways with some 18,000 people who work there and thousands more residents who come on public business.

It has grown so bad in the past year that county workers continually call for increased protection. Members of the public express shock at what they call Third World conditions.

Crime statistics show violence is increasing. Homeless activists say contagious diseases are spreading. And no one is at greater risk than the homeless themselves.

Police admit how tough it is to make much headway.

All this has led the Santa Ana City Council to consider declaring a public health and safety crisis in an ordinance council members will take up Tuesday.

Tensions at the Civic Center ratcheted up Aug. 1, when police shot a homeless man during an altercation outside the county courthouse. Richard Gene Swihart, 32, died two weeks later from his wounds.

Both the city and the county have stepped up efforts to help fix the growing problems at the Civic Center. But workers question

the sense of urgency among administrators and elected officials who don't have to walk through the plaza to get to their offices.

"The executives park under the building and take an elevator up," said Jennifer Muir Beuthin, general manager for Orange County Employees Association.

"They're not confronted with the same thing every day that rank-and-file workers are confronted with when they're walking through the encampment."

Perpetrators and Victims

To someone like Anna Mae "Mama Brizy" Gonzalez, a homeless woman who has slept at the Civic Center the past nine years, change can't happen soon enough.

Slowed by triple bypass surgery last year, the 66-year-old Gonzalez said that when she first arrived at Civic Center, things were calmer. There were fewer transients and fewer severe mental and behavioral problems. And there was less violence.

"We have 5150s," she said, using street slang for the mentally ill who need to be hospitalized. "Then you've got people who really don't want to listen."

A mid-August survey by county workers recorded a 14 percent increase in the area's homeless population, up from 406 to 461 people, over the past year. Most of those people can be found in a 1-square-mile area between Broadway and Flower Street, bounded by Santa Ana Boulevard and Civic Center Drive.

The population surge has come during a long-term jump in crime. From 2011 to 2015, the number of assaults with a deadly weapon in the Civic Center nearly quadrupled and robberies grew almost threefold, according to Santa Ana police records.

Gonzales said dope is everywhere, drawing people from surrounding neighborhoods and making it harder for the homeless to keep the peace among themselves.

Santa Ana Police Chief Carlos Rojas said the Police Department is limited in what it can enforce. Officers can patrol and make

arrests on charges of drug possession, violent behavior and public indecency or can issue tickets for illegal camping.

But Rojas said it's not illegal to be homeless; they have civil liberties and rights governing their possessions. The police, he added, try to treat them with dignity.

"We understand that these people need services. At the same time, we're trying to balance that with the public safety.

"It's not an easy job."

Fear and Danger

On seven occasions in February, county employees at the Civic Center requested that sheriff's deputies escort them to their cars after work. They were too fearful to walk alone through the darkness of winter's early evening hours.

That same month, just outside the county courthouse, Santa Ana police arrested a 55-year-old man accused of using a 4-foot-long wooden stick to beat his girlfriend in the back and bludgeon another person in the head. He also was found with methamphetamine, police said.

Records from the county and City of Santa Ana make it clear: Though public employees routinely feel unsafe and occasionally are accosted at the Civic Center, the victims of violent crime there are almost always homeless people.

Last year, 23 aggravated assaults and 20 robberies were reported in the Civic Center, according to Santa Ana police. Homeless people were by far the chief victims.

And since 2011, at least six women have reported being raped at the Civic Center – most of them waking up during an assault or discovering evidence of an attack after a deep or intoxicated sleep.

Advocates suspect assaults are much higher than what is reported to police.

"We've gotten quite a few reports of rapes. It's almost like it's happening weekly," said Paul Leon, founder and chief executive of Illumination Foundation, an Irvine-based nonprofit that works with the homeless.

"Most of the women down there will tell you (they've) been at least fondled or (their) clothes have been ripped off."

But he and others said homeless victims often don't report a crime because they feel dismissed by the police.

Gonzalez said she and other homeless people routinely are ignored by the Santa Ana police unit that is permanently assigned to patrol the Civic Center, though she admits the homeless community sometimes adopts a "don't snitch" attitude.

"We would call police and they don't come out," Gonzalez said, adding that the police tell them "anything that goes on at night, you have to handle it."

Police Chief Rojas denied that officers ignore complaints. He said rampant drug use and mental illness in the homeless population can make proving some cases difficult. But, contradicting what others say, Rojas contended his officers have been successful in gathering information and gaining trust at the Civic Center. '

"We encourage them to call the police, and if someone was telling them otherwise, that would not be appropriate," Rojas said. "It's not something we would ignore or not investigate."

In 2012, the department formed the Homeless Evaluation Assessment Response Team – a program that teaches officers to track individuals among the homeless and try to refer them to the services they might need.

"We can't arrest ourselves out of homelessness," Rojas said. "Just like we can't arrest ourselves out of crime."

It's not as though public officials have sat idly as the homeless population boomed.

In the past year, the county has bought an Anaheim warehouse to convert into the first countywide, year-round homeless shelter, hired a director to coordinate the county's services for the homeless, stationed a special sheriff's officer on a main walkway and received a grant for new mental health facilities.

On Thursday, county Supervisor Andrew Do proposed moving quickly on a longstanding goal of converting a nearby former bus terminal into a permanent shelter.

For its part, the city has increased power washing in the area, approved a project to convert a local motel into 71 new dwellings for the chronically homeless and will consider stepping up police patrols and code enforcement.

But government employees don't feel enough is being done to ensure their safety.

Intimidation and Disruption

Civic Center workers have reported being attacked near their workplaces at least seven times in the past two years. A log of 194 county employee complaints details many of those attacks.

Those include: a woman punching a county worker in her head; a man charging a Public Defender's Office investigator; a woman attacking a Santa Ana police meter worker and a county intern in a parking lot; and a man leaping onto a sheriff's special officer after being discovered hiding in a government office service closet.

Employees also complain of people shooting heroin in public bathrooms, brawling near building entrances, challenging pedestrians to fights, intimidating and following workers, hiding behind cars in the parking lot and exposing their genitals.

One man even was seen stalking another with a pickax.

Apprehension among workers and others at the Civic Center has grown to the point that it's disrupting some civic business.

In May, Orange County Superior Court CEO Alan Carlson wrote a letter to county supervisors and Santa Ana City Council members saying jurors have asked to serve in county courthouses elsewhere and that the staff doen't want to work past 5 p.m. "because of the homeless encampment that is engulfing the courthouse."

Alan Clow, a senior investigator with the Orange County Public Defender's Office and an OCEA board member, said secretaries in his office don't go out to lunch anymore. And attorneys have stopped coming to the office on weekends to prep for Monday jury trials.

"You have to be on guard when you go out there because anything can happen," Clow said. "I tell them walk in numbers. I didn't have to do that three or four years ago."

The county has made some security upgrades – increasing the number of sheriff's special officers who are stationed at county buildings, performing perimeter checks and escorting employees to their vehicles after work.

Another part of the county's interim solution: Asking employees to learn to protect themselves.

On Wednesday, at an employee safety training, a Sheriff's Department slideshow advised workers to take elevators instead of stairwells, to "walk tall" and "express confident body language" and to stay on busy streets, avoiding shortcuts.

They were also told how to respond to an attacker with a gun vs. a knife – and what to do if an altercation can't be avoided.

"Strike first, strike hard, strike as many times as you can ... (in) the eyes and nose" and "end the fight as quickly as possible," the department advised.

Lezlee Neebe, a veteran courtroom clerk who goes to the Central Justice Center three times a week, said Superior Court employees were given permission a few months ago to begin carrying pepper spray.

"Why should employees even need to carry pepper spray to work?" Neebe asked. "I have compassion for the homeless, but it has grown to the point where you can't avoid it."

Rules and Disregard

Gonzalez, whose nickname comes from her maiden name of Briseño, is looked upon as a "street mother" who provides leadership in her makeshift community.

"The young people that are coming in here, a lot of them don't know there's rules to follow," she said.

She's talking about rules the homeless establish among themselves to maintain some sense of civility.

Gonzalez also wishes drug users would throw away used syringes, pointing to a brown needle disposal container sitting atop a low concrete wall.

Instead, more needles – many handed out as part of a health program aimed at preventing the spread of HIV and hepatitis C – end up on the ground.

"We had a member who stepped on a used syringe and it stuck in their shoe," said Muir Beuthin, whose union represents more than 10,000 county workers.

During an early-morning walking tour of the Civic Center, she peered over a small concrete railing that borders the Superior Court building. At least two dozen used syringes were on the ground, many with caps off and needles exposed.

It's always like this, according to Muir Beuthin. Sixty feet away, another seven needles lay exposed on landscaping alongside a well-traversed path outside an area called the Plaza of Flags.

"Regularly, our members have to step over feces and urine and drug paraphernalia when they're coming to work. The public has to do that, too, when they're coming to get birth or marriage certificates or pay their taxes."

The Santa Ana Central Library, one of two serving a city of more than 340,000 and the only one with full services, has been hit particularly hard. The award-winning civic institution recently reopened after a two-week hiatus to redesign the ground floor, changes made mainly to handle the many homeless people who seek refuge. Signs in the library restroom ask visitors not to bathe, shave or wash items.

The library also increased the number of security guards from one to four. It also hired a contractor, at a cost of about $20,000 a year, to clean the restrooms repeatedly throughout the day. Before, when cleaning took place only once in the morning, restrooms had to be closed by 11 a.m. as they were such a mess, said Heather Folmar, library operations manager.

About the same time the library closed temporarily, the county installed three portable toilets, open 24 hours, on Ross Street near

a construction site that displaced some homeless people from their Civic Center spots. Those toilets, heavily used by the homeless, are expected to remain.

Folmar said people camped at the Civic Center when she started working at the library 25 years ago. Today, she said, it's 20 times worse.

"I don't blame the homeless; they have no alternative," Folmar said. "Where are they to go? Where are they to sleep? Where are they to take a shower?"

Health and Hygiene

The lack of facilities for the homeless to practice the most basic hygiene can have deadly results.

Illumination Foundation staffers, who are at the Civic Center every day, hear about and see suspected cases of various infections that include E. coli, Clostridium difficile or C. diff and the antibiotic-resistant MRSA.

"It really is a silent epidemic," said nonprofit founder Leon.

Leon remembers one call about a man whose open sores caused consternation among other homeless people at the Civic Center. Leon and staff couldn't find him until someone pointed out the man at a nearby fast-food restaurant, where he had just handed the cashier money for a drink.

When the man pulled up his sleeves and pants legs, "It was probably the worst case of MRSA I've ever seen," Leon said. "It was to the bone."

A bacterium, MRSA is spread by contact. The Illumination Foundation got the man to UCI Medical Center, where he died two months later.

But since 2011, the only Civic Center outbreak recorded by the county Health Care Agency came in 2013, a cluster of eight cases of Shigella, a gastrointestinal illness that causes fever and diarrhea.

The Health Care Agency does not do any formal surveillance in the Civic Center other than as part of countywide tracking of specific diseases, such as influenza, that are required by state

law to be reported, said Dr. Matthew Zahn, the county's medical director of epidemiology and assessment.

But county public health nurses regularly walk at the Civic Center, Zahn said, mostly to educate the homeless on illness prevention and to address self-reported health problems.

Social workers and mental health workers from the county also cruise the Civic Center to assess the needs of the homeless and direct them to services. They greet people with clipboards in hand and do intake from a mobile unit parked weekly on the mall.

"The reality is the reason our staff is there is because that population is at a higher risk for health issues," Zahn said.

"A lot of germs we talk about may spread through that community."

Madeleine Spencer, a member of Project Homelessness Coalition, said outbreaks of the flu and staph infections regularly sweep through the Civic Center.

The county, Spencer said, provides insufficient health care to address communicable diseases that can spread beyond the homeless community.

"If someone is touching a doorknob, your workers are all going to get it, too."

Cleaning offers only temporary relief, said Neebe, the courtroom clerk.

"They can power-wash and clean," she said, "but it's there again by the next morning."

For now, workers, the public and the homeless must coexist.

Albert Torres, a friend of "Brizy" Gonzalez, has a tattoo across his chest that reads, "Only God Can Judge Me." Torres, 45, another leader in the Civic Center, said much fear could be eased if other people stopped to talk to the homeless.

"I think it's exaggerated," Torres said, "because they don't know us."

Spending Time in Prison Increases the Risk of Becoming Homeless

Shelter Scotland

Shelter Scotland is a UK based organization that campaigns to help and prevent homelessness.

Foreword

It is well documented and widely accepted that spending time in prison increases an individual's chances of becoming homeless. Prisoners who have problems securing accommodation on their release are significantly more likely to reoffend than those individuals who do not face these challenges.

This assertion is borne out through official statistics which show that in 2014/15, 6% of statutory homeless applications in Scotland came from people leaving prison[1] , a significant over representation against national demographics, and that 30% of those released from prison do not know where they are going to live on their liberation[2] . In addition, two thirds of those who were homeless after their release from prison go on to reoffend[3] and research has shown a reduction in recidivism of as much as 20% for those who had stable accommodation on their release compared to those who do not [4] .

These stark figures are set against a current prison population of 7,500 in Scotland, but an annual liberation rate of nearly 20,000, due to the fact that a large proportion of prisoners are in custody for short periods of time. Of those that are liberated, one third have served less than 12 months and 44% are released from remand. Of the 19,792 prisoners liberated in 2011-12, 8,787 had been on remand and 6,548 were sentenced to less than a year.[5] Due to the short period in custody there is less time to engage with support agencies and evidence has shown that these groups are even more prone to homelessness.[6]

"Preventing Homelessness and Reducing Reoffending," Shelter Scotland, 2015. Reprinted by permission.

The fact that there are up to 300% more liberations in Scotland annually than there are prisoners in custody, underlines the central importance of ensuring that there is a consistent approach to supporting prisoners in accessing suitable housing on their release.

Shelter Scotland has been providing services in prisons for over 15 years and contribute to a wider patchwork of provision across the country at present. Despite significant national investment in Through the Gate services provided by statutory, charitable and private sector providers, it is a recognised challenge that services at the front end are patchy and inconsistent across Scotland.

Over the last two decades, there has been significant focus on the development of services for people as they leave prison to help address some of the root causes that link reoffending and homelessness. In recent years, public policy work and practice development has moved towards a focus on the themes of co-production and early prevention to address the root causes of reoffending and homelessness, driven principally by the need to reduce national expenditure and deliver better value and outcomes in this area.

This approach has been supported by a welcome emphasis and commitment from the Scottish Prison Service (SPS) to the provision of both internal and external rehabilitative support through their ThroughCare Services. This, combined with ambitious Homelessness legislation in Scotland which remains the most progressive in Europe, offers an environment and an expectation for the link between homelessness and reoffending to become less of an issue.

We need to better understand why, despite investment and undoubted commitment and efforts in this field, the link between reoffending and homelessness in Scotland remains alarmingly evident.

Understanding lived experience is the foundation stone of any genuine approach to the delivery of co-produced services and Shelter Scotland has sought the views of people who have been in prison to directly inform this report and our recommendations.

As a practitioner in this area, Shelter Scotland has sought the experiences of those with whom we have worked directly through the Supporting Prisoners; Advice Network (SPAN) Scotland – a joint initiative between Shelter Scotland, Sacro and Inverness Citizens Advice Bureau focused on tackling homelessness among ex-offenders and reducing reoffending.

The results of the research are presented in this report structured around the key themes that emerged from these interviews. This direct insight, combined with our existing research and practice experience are used to develop a series of recommendations for future policy and practice work to improve the housing outcomes for people on release from prison.

1. Introduction

The strong, complicated and reciprocal links between offending and homelessness are well known and evidenced. Spending time in prison increases the risk of homelessness as many people lose their tenancy whilst they are in prison, or find themselves unwelcome to return to their previous household on release.[7]

There are limited housing options for people who have become homeless whilst in prison, with long waiting lists and limited choices in the social rented sector, and significant financial and attitudinal barriers to the private rented market.[8] Many prison leavers who have applied as homeless to their local authority will spend considerable periods in temporary accommodation, such as hostels.[9] At the most extreme end, some people leave prison and have no choice but to sleep rough.[10] A lack of stable accommodation increases the likelihood of reoffending.[11] A self-perpetuating negative cycle of moving between homelessness and prison can develop.[12]

The risk of homelessness for people leaving prison was recognised in the 2002 Homelessness Task Force recommendations, which called for those responsible for prisoners to develop high quality homelessness and housing advice services.[13] They are also recognised as a group at high risk by the Prevention of

Homelessness Guidance, which points to processes and staff knowledge that should be in place to respond appropriately to prison leavers.[14] Since publishing the Guidance in 2009, there has been a strong focus at a Scottish Government level on homelessness prevention, which is integral to the 'housing options' approach that local authorities are required to adopt.

Likewise, from the justice perspective the issue of homelessness has been long identified as a contributing factor to reoffending. For example, the (then) Scottish Executive's National Strategy for Management of Offenders (2006) identified 'the ability to access and sustain suitable accommodation' as one of the nine offender outcomes.[15]

The Christie Commission further highlighted the importance of prevention and the importance of investing in prevention activities across public services in order not only to save personal crises but also as an effective way to save public money.[16]

Despite the above, there remains a substantial number of people every year that leave prison in Scotland with nowhere to call home.

2,108 homeless applications came from people leaving prison in 2014/15,[17] although this figure is unlikely to represent the full scale of the problem, particularly when this figure is reviewed against Scottish Government statistics showing that nearly 20,000 people are liberated from prison each year. Research shows that 30% of people liberated do not have a home to go to[18] so of the 20,000 people liberated, up to 6,000 people without a home might provide a truer representation. It is clear that there is still much that could be done to fully adopt a preventative approach to tackling homelessness and reoffending.

In Scotland there has recently been a renewed interest in understanding and addressing the issue of housing and homelessness for prison leavers. For example:

- Audit Scotland's report on Reducing Reoffending in Scotland (2012) highlighted that access to housing is a particular issue for people leaving prison, that many ex-offenders experienced

homelessness and that housing support for offenders is not consistent across Scotland

- The Ministerial Working Group on the ReIntegration of Offenders established and selected housing as its first theme, subsequently commissioning further research into the issue (October 2013)
- 'Improving Housing Options for Offenders' pilot as part of the Reducing Reoffending II programme (January 2014)
- The appointment by Scottish Prisons Service of a Policy Manager for housing and welfare (2014)
- The upcoming Criminal Justice (Scotland) Bill that will reshape services for prisoners' integration into the community and has identified housing as one of the crucial factors for successful rehabilitation.

In addition, the current Scottish Prison Service (SPS) mission focuses on "providing services that help to transform the lives of people in our care so they can fulfil their potential and become responsible citizens".[19] The SPS' strategic commitment to develop a personcentred approach, working together with partners to support re-integration on their release, ties well with their commitment to the prevention of reoffending by taking steps to focus on the full journey through and out of custody and back into the community.

Shelter Scotland has had a dedicated service working with prisoners to prevent homelessness since 1999. Currently, we deliver the Supporting Prisoners; Advice Network (SPAN) Scotland project in partnership with Sacro and Inverness Citizens Advice Bureau, funded by the Big Lottery. Since its inception in 2013, SPAN has worked with over 1,600 people across 3 prisons; HMP Perth, Grampian and Inverness. The SPAN project focuses on prevention of homelessness by assisting people in custody to maintain their current home where possible as well as working with people to ensure that they have a home when they leave prison.

SPAN has been committed to working with prisoners to meaningfully support the move from prison into the community. The service's most significant learnings and developments have

resulted from discussions with those people who have used the service, including the development of Peer Learning.

This report provides an opportunity for the stories and opinions of people who have been in prison to be heard, using their own words. It aims to bring together practitioner and service user opinion, coupled with examples showcasing some of the services that have evolved as a result of the views and experiences of people in prison.

This report concludes by making a range of recommendations that, if implemented, Shelter Scotland believes would contribute to improving the housing outcomes for people on release from prison. The recommendations are divided between strategic issues and the promotion of good practice on the ground. To see real change effected in the reduction of reoffending it is crucial that both strategic frameworks and practical implementation prioritise the prevention of homelessness for prisoners.

2. Methodology

In April 2015 we conducted interviews with 16 people that the SPAN project has worked with.

Using a semi-structured interview technique, we asked questions about where they had been living, what had happened to their housing whilst they were in prison and what was going to happen/ had happened when they were liberated. We also asked about the work that SPAN had done with them and what would have happened if that help hadn't been available. A full list of the questions can be found in Appendix A. Notes were taken during each interview to capture the main points that were being expressed and where possible (9 out of 16), interviews were also recorded.[20]

Two researchers independently reviewed all available notes and audio recordings and a thematic analysis of the interviews is presented in section 4 of this report.

In answer to both the direct question about how SPAN had worked with the interviewees and also throughout responses to other questions, information was collected about the work that

SPAN has undertaken to prevent homelessness. This information is presented in section 5.

Throughout the report, where appropriate, evidence from a literature review of existing research and Shelter Scotland's own research has been drawn upon to further inform this report.

Interviewees

Interviewees had been approached by SPAN staff to participate in the research with a view to the sample being representative of the range of the experiences and challenges that their wider group of service users face. This included two relatives of people who were in prison, as this is a significant part of SPAN's work. Interviewees were marked (A) to (P) and throughout this report, when evidence has been drawn or quoted from an interview it has been referenced using this key to protect the anonymity of interviewees.

3. Themes

Two researchers independently reviewed all available notes and audio recordings from the interviews and each identified the themes they assessed as most prominent. There was a high level of correlation in the thematic analysis and through discussion based on the evidence; eight themes were selected as encompassing the most important issues to the interviewees.

Theme 1: Importance of house as home

Housing problems and solutions were not just about the practical concerns of retaining accommodation. A theme that clearly came through in the interviews was the idea of a house as a 'home'. The aspects of housing as a 'home' raised in the research can be grouped into three categories.

Home as a source of pride and investment

"when I thought I was gonna lose the hoose I was depressed – I made it nice, cleaned it and that...I know I've got a chance now " (N)

"I've had my wee hoose and that for about 15 year and I kinda, it's taken us ages and ages to get it done up and I'm kinda getting it done up the way I want to get it done up, making it my own home"(A)

"I had done the flat up smart and didn't want to lose it" (L)

"having a foundation has changed me, it's my own thing to have responsibility for " (N)

Having support close by, and knowing the neighbours

"It's just my house, I've been there for so long now I'm just used to being there. It's only a bedsit but it's my wee bedsit eh so… and it's close to my mum and everything " (G)

"We all know everybody and it's a kinda safe place and that for everybody " (A)

"I've got it set up the way I want it to be an that…and my neighbours doesnae bother us, I speak to them in passing, there's nae noise on the landing, it's a good place " (B)

"having a foundation has changed me, it's my own thing to have responsibility for " (N)

The home as safe and enabling

"I don't really know what it would mean if I did lose my house, I'd probably stay back at my mum's house and I'm 34 years of age and I kinda want to have a kid and things " (A)

"That's my ain sanctuary, I can dae what I want in my house, watch what I want, go to my bed, come and go as I please " (B)

"I had done the flat up smart and didn't want to lose it " (L)

"[my flat] gives me a base…don't want to go through the homeless route again. I'm 36 now and too old to be bouncing around "(P)

One interviewee who had been placed in temporary accommodation for over 2 months commented

> "it wouldn't be so bad if I could even paint the living room ken, just so dull…I keep getting telt to move on, move on…It's over a year and a half since I've been in a home…I want somewhere I can call mine". (H)

The importance of having a home, as described above, was also linked to previous experience, where people had spent long periods in temporary accommodation or on waiting lists and the fear that this would happen again. One interviewee who had previously been on waiting lists for eight years commented:

> "took us ages to get it ken. Then I almost lost it ken, because of this. It's just pure stupidness." (C)

> "it's took me ages to get my house and to go back into a homeless again with nae nothing…and to need to start off again with the clothes that are on your back when you're coming out the jail…" (D)

This concern around the alternative and losing the home was linked to a fear of hostels, which is analysed as a separate theme later in this document.

Theme 2: Belongings

Connected to the theme of home, some of the interviewees also talked about the importance of their belongings. Several talked about their fear that they would lose their possessions whilst in custody if their tenancy was ended. This echoes findings from larger, broader research into the experience of prisoners that also found that loss of possessions was a common experience and barrier to rehabilitation for prisoners.[21]

> "If she [girlfriend] hadn't been there they would probably have changed the locks and put my stuff in storage " (A)

"I would have lost my house and everything in it … all my valuables and things like that … the important things … maybe no to anybody else … photos of my bairns " (D)

"My flat's lovely… you don't know if all your stuff is gonna be thrown out on the street " (O)

One interviewee was concerned not about his own, but his mum's possessions, as she passed away while he was in custody and the local authority were asking him to sign over his rights to succession (F). The emotional distress caused to him by thinking about his mum's possessions being discarded was significant. This issue has been identified and actioned upon by SPAN through their work, including establishing a relationship with a local church in the area who agreed to store belongings at no cost.

Theme 3: Importance of Friends and Family
8 of 14 people interviewed who were or had been in custody mentioned the positive support and practical assistance they received from those on the "outside". This is further evidenced by the fact that in 2014, 14% of all SPAN cases involved engagement with the families and friends of those in custody to help prevent homelessness on their release. This theme was very important for the people we interviewed both in terms of knowing that there was someone looking out for them, and in the impact that their actions had in preventing eviction. In the interviews this support fell into four categories:

Occupying the property
One of the tools used by SPAN to prevent the end of a tenancy is to negotiate and organise for somebody else to occupy the property for the period that the service user is in prison. For two of the interviewees a 'qualifying occupier' had been found and accepted by the landlord. This person is usually a partner or friend. There needs to be trust in this situation as a level of responsibility remains with the original tenant. Sub-letting or creating a joint tenancy can also be options, and one of the interviewees was exploring whether

either of these could be possible in his case (A). Indeed, interviewee A who had been in and out of prison for years expressed that he was quite used to relying on friends and family to take on his tenancy for the times he has been in custody.

Paying towards rent arrears

In three cases (I, K, P), interviewees reported that their mothers were paying a weekly amount towards rent arrears as a 'good will gesture'. This had been negotiated and organised by SPAN staff with landlords in order to prevent eviction. In another case, there was an arrangement for financial help on release, "When I get out my mum and dad are going to help [pay back rent arrears], without them I'd be stuck" (O).

Practical help

Through the interviews we learnt of several ways in which family had supported people who were in prison in practical ways regarding their home. The mum that we interviewed mentioned that she had been checking her son's flat every day and was looking after the gas and electric accounts to reduce the risk of jeopardising the tenancy when the qualifying occupier moved in (I). In another case, the interviewee's mum had been going into the house to check for post and had found a letter from the landlord threatening eviction, which had spurred the daughter to get in touch with SPAN (K). Another interviewee mentioned that his brother was looking after his belongings whilst he was in prison (M).

Desire to remain living near family support

Some of the interviewees mentioned how important it was for them to live close to family support when they got out of prison. This correlates with research that has shown that finding accommodation close to positive social networks can reduce reoffending behaviour[22] and is also key to preventing recurring homelessness.[23] One of the interviewees said that they would want to move to a smaller property but "it's got to be the right move – in the area near my family" (F).

Conversely, three people discussed the impact of not having support on the outside from family or friends. Interviewee P spoke strongly from his experience of having been in custody several times about people without a supportive network to go to when they leave prison, "People who haven't got a house and are isolated, when they're going to leave, they say, like, 'I'll do a crime and be back next week'. In this day and age it shouldn't be like that" (P). The impact of isolation is a contributory factor in reoffending as prison can offer familiarity and a sense of community. Ignoring this basic human need is to ignore a causal link between housing and reoffending.

Theme 4: The Right Home Helps Prevent Reoffending

For many of those interviewed (13 out of 16), a home was considered to be essential as a foundation to help reduce the likelihood of reoffending. This reflects the findings of previous research that has shown prisoners to have concerns about reoffending in relation to housing prospects. For example, one large scale longitudinal study that found that 60% of prisoners believed that having a place to live would help them to stop offending.[24]

Home as a source of pride

There were two strands to this highlighted in the interviews. The first centred on the home as a source of pride that could motivate individuals to change their behaviour. Home was seen as something to work towards, to set down foundations be near family members, and take on other tasks such as volunteering, all of which it was felt that would help them not reoffend.

> "it would really help if I could keep my house an' that and I do really think it'd keep me on the straight and narrow..." (A)

> "I would've been back in here again...Coz when I had no furniture and no electric I just felt lost out there eh. And if I get my furniture and my electric on I'm gonna brighten up my ideas. I wanna get some voluntary work or something " (E)

"he's been trying because he was proud of his house and his job… Knowing about the house keeps him going – …when he thought he was going to be losing his house he was self-harming " (I)

"Having a foundation has changed me, it's my own thing to have responsibility …I know I've got a chance now…keeping my house has made me want to change " (N)

Unsuitable Accommodation

The second strand that emerged was the flip side of the above – that is, a belief that if they did not have a home, they may end up in unsuitable accommodation within an environment which led to reoffending. Generally, this relates to a fear of hostels and the negative impact on offending that interviewees feared hostels would have. (See theme 5)

Two interviewees who were currently on the housing waiting list highlighted the importance of the location of accommodation, with one saying they had told the council they didn't want to be put in an area with drug users: "feart in case something happens and I get put back inside" (H). Another interviewee had requested to move area for this same reason: "I'd just end up back in here all the time…because of people in the area I go about with" (C). These concerns are well-founded: research has shown that relationships with anti-social associates has been described as 'one of the most potent predictors of reoffending'.[26]

One interviewee commented that he had seen many people who did not have a home to be released to reoffend for the purpose of returning to the prison, "When they're going to leave, they say, like, 'I'll do a crime and I'll be back next week'" (P). Although none of the interview cohort expressed this as their own intention, other research has also found that some prison leavers feel driven to reoffend in order to return to the secure 'accommodation' of prison.[27] This clearly demonstrates that releasing a prisoner without them having a secure home to go to runs counter to the purposes of prison rehabilitation, and the Scottish Prison Service's mission

to reduce reoffending by transforming the lives of people in their care.[28]

Theme 5: Fear of Hostels

Of the 14 interviews with people who had experienced custody, 9 mentioned having spent time previously in a hostel.[29] Of the 9 interviews that mentioned spending time in hostels, 7 talked about not wanting to return to a hostel. One other, whom it was not clear from the interview whether they had been in a hostel previously, was also adamant that they would not want to spend time in one. This concern has been evidenced in other, larger scale, pieces of research.[30] The Homelessness Task Force noted in 2002[31] that many can get caught in a cycle of prison – hostel – prison, and this was a pattern that had been experienced by some of the interviewees. Research for the Scottish Government also reports increasing consensus that rehousing prison leavers in mainstream rather than hostel accommodation will reduce reoffending.[32]

Several interviewees gave specific reasons for wanting to avoid time in a hostel. Across all reasoning, it can be seen from the quotes below that most often the root of the concern was being placed in circumstances that could lead to reoffending. The experiences and opinions expressed demonstrate that for prisoners to be accommodated in hostels post-release runs contrary to the Scottish Government's prevention agenda, which has been promoted in both the spheres of homelessness and community justice. Indeed, if the fears about hostels expressed by the interviewees were realized, this practice could be seen as a key contributing factor to reoffending behaviour.

Alcohol/Drugs

For several interviewees, the thought of going into a hostel brought on fears of a drug or alcohol related relapse.

> "Before I got my hoose I refused to go into a homeless hostel, because I'm stable on methadone and I didn't want to go back the

way… I've been in there before and you've got people chapping on your door like you got this, you got that, you got any drugs, nut " (B)

"[Without SPAN] I'd have went back to hostels, got drinking, been back in [prison] again quick " (M)

"They will find you somewhere [through the homeless route] but it's maybe not suitable for you – like a hostel, you'll relapse into drugs n' that then go back to prison. It's costing the country money too " (P)

Loss of freedom
The loss of freedom associated with being in a hostel, in comparison to other accommodation types, was brought up in discussions.

"In a house I can come and go as please and do what I want [in contrast to hostel] " (B)

"It took me ages to get a home and I wouldn't want to go back to having nothing in homeless places " (D)

Expense
In some cases, a concern over the cost of hostels and how a service user would finance this was raised.

"I would have had to steal to pay for homeless hostels " (D)

"It's hard to work and be in a hostel and get yourself straight because the hostels are so expensive " (M)

Association with people who are a bad influence
For other interviewees, not wanting to go into a hostel was attributed to other residents and interviewees concerns about their own actions if they came into contact with them.

"I didnae wanna go to the hostels coz that'd be bad, it's like a prison really – it's hard to explain – it's like the people that are

in there – some people are different – that's the last place I'd want to go " (F)

"The homeless unit and the jail, they're kinda like the same place… I would have ended up in the homeless unit, seeing someone I don't like – getting into trouble " (G)

One interviewee also spoke about his experience in a B&B as restrictive, although preferable to a hostel. Interviewee H was in a B&B for 5 ½ months, which he found depressing. The only cooking facility was a microwave, there were no washing facilities: "I couldn't even really buy milk as it would go off by the end of the day." (H)

Theme 6: *Stress and Depression*

13 out of 16 interviewees explicitly talked about experiencing stress or depression in relation to their housing situation whilst they were in prison. The other three interviewees implied similar feelings through their tone of voice and the way that they spoke about housing, but didn't name their feelings during the interviews.

Although it is possible to assume that those who were stressed or depressed about housing would be more likely to access SPAN, one of the interviewees commented that in his experience of being in the prison halls, "About 90% of people in here would say that housing is the thing that is most on their mind" (P), which could suggest that housing is a very common cause of stress among the prison population.

The cause of the worry and depression discussed could be split into three main categories:

Fear of losing home

At the root of any anxiety interviewees had about not knowing what was going to happen was the fear of losing their home, as well as a fear of becoming homeless or staying in a homeless hostel.

"The arrears started building up when I went into jail – I was worrying, worrying, worrying… " (G)

"He has some emotional, mental difficulties…when he thought he was going to be losing his house he was self-harming." (I)

Not knowing what is going to happen

Many of the interviewees referred to a strong sense of not knowing about the systems and rules that decide what happens to them. This uncertainty was a significant cause of stress for some of the people we spoke to:

"I was wary of what was going to happen …I didn't know if I could keep it … I'm worried and just keep thinking about it " (E)

"The house was the main worry. I was panicking because I didn't know what would happen about the Housing Benefit " (O)

"It was a worry off my mind… I've seen so many lassies lost their flats " (K)

"When I first came in I was panicky, agitated and worried before I knew what was happening with the house " (L)

This last statement from interviewee L highlights that the stress of not knowing what is going to happen to your home can not only effect mental health but that this, in turn, can impact prisoners' behaviour.

Agitated prisoners will absorb more prison staff time and resources, as well as potentially negatively impact the behaviour of other prisoners around them.

Waiting

Four prisoners spoke about the time between going into prison and feeling reassured because SPAN was proactively working with them.

"The time in between getting the letters and talking to Pam was difficult – I'd almost given up " (G)

"It was 3 ½ months before I spoke to Becky – that was a long time to feel worried " K)

"SPAN was a great help, a piece of mind – but I had to wait a month to see her " (O)

"Sometimes by the time you get seen your house is gone " (P)

Based on the stress that they had experienced whilst waiting, the clear message from several interviews was that advice and support would be welcomed as soon as possible once entering the prison.

The majority of responses to Question 4, 'what else would have helped?' were suggestions about how advice could be accessed more quickly. This reflects much of the literature that exists around this topic, which acknowledges that the assessment of housing need should start as soon as possible in order to enable a tenancy to be maintained or planning for resettlement.[33]

However, one prisoner (N) shared a helpful insight into his heightened emotional state when entering the prison and suggested that questions about housing at the core screening can be too soon after being committed to be helpful or incur an accurate response. Core screening is an assessment meeting which takes place within the first 72 hours designed to identify the immediate needs of all prisoners across a range of areas.[34]

"They shouldn't ask you those [core screen] questions straight away – your head's all messed up – stressed away – You've been in the court cells, greetin', punching the walls. It's a couple of weeks until you can think straight. " (N)

Theme 7: Lack of knowledge

One of the most frequently used phrases during the interviews was "I didn't know". When people used this phrase they were often talking about issues such as housing benefit rules, housing rights (e.g. social housing transfers, succession) and the homelessness application process.

"I'm not clever with things like that, I'm just pure stupit about things like that– it's hard, ken? " (C)

"Rent arrears were going up and up and I didnae know what to do about that" (D)

"The amount of people in the halls that d'nae ken where they are wi' their hoose..." (F)

"It's actually quite fine for me to know that there's somebody on the end of the phone that I can actually speak to that can help me through things because I havenae a clue" (I)

Many of the interviewees had been told about the help that the SPAN project could give them by people in their hall who had previously benefitted from the project. One of the interviewees mentioned that they would do likewise: "If I knew someone was in the same situation I would be able to tell them where to go coz I've had some brilliant help" (G).

Unfortunately, sometimes the sharing of knowledge between prisoners can also be unhelpful when the information is not accurate, or not universally applicable. This was mentioned a few times during the interviews. For example, a common misconception shared in prisons is that everyone gets 13 weeks of housing benefit paid, whereas in reality this is only true for prisoners sentenced to under 6 months. Another rumour was that unless you stay in a hostel you cannot be assessed as homeless (P). This wrong knowledge can be more damaging to successful housing outcomes than no knowledge at all. An absence of universally available, accurate prevention advice to counter poor information can either result in complacency, with prisoners assuming that everything will be alright and then losing their tenancy, or in resources needing to be used more intensively to put right any damage done.

Three interviewees felt that prison officers had not been available as a source of information or help around housing.

"Some of the prison officers don't know how it works with housing ... some of them don't care" (G)/ "Naebody [prison officers] told me nothing. One of the girls from the halls said go and see Becky" (K).

All of the people who commented on this felt that that would have liked prison officers to be more informed about housing and the specialist agencies that are available for prisoners. Interviewees also suggested that leaflets/ forms for housing and housing benefit being available in halls and a greater availability of SPAN staff would help prisoners with their lack of knowledge.

Educating prisoners on housing is one of the aims of SPAN, who have provided information sessions for people in prison. These have proven very successful with over 150 people attending over a 6 month period. The commitment to sharing knowledge within the prison is evidenced through the "Insiders Project", a co-production initiative developed between SPAN and prisoners which provided training in housing to volunteers within the prison who then acted as Peer Mentors, supported by SPAN. This has been developed further to include SQA accreditation, creating a qualification for the volunteer with the aim to help support individual development and reintegration upon release.

Theme 8: Communication with professionals

The impact of poor communication within and across agencies was raised by many of the interviewees. Communication from landlords about tenancies had frequently been unhelpful and unclear for the recipients. Issues around poor communication were often exacerbated by the prisoner's confinement.

Interviewees spoke of confusing language being used in letters regarding their tenancies, thought by some to be deliberately misleading or worded in a way that promoted the best interests of the landlord rather than laying out all the different options available to the tenant. In many instances this was a letter asking interviewees to sign over their tenancies because they were in custody, worded in a way that made it sound as though this was the only or best course of action.

> "I got letters and that off [housing association] and that and it was a mandate letter or something like that saying if I fill this in if I want to give my hoose up, and I started panicking" (A)

There was also a common issue of requests being made of prisoners by agencies that they felt unable to fulfil when they were in prison. An example of this was a letter sent to the prison requesting that the interviewee visit the office to discuss the issue (P), an action that would clearly be impossible for anyone in custody.

In some instances, the letters were sent to the original address, and interviewees had to rely on friends or family passing these on to them. In some examples the landlord was aware the interviewee was in custody and indeed that was the basis of the letter. For example, Interviewee J, whose partner was in custody, received correspondence to the flat in her partner's name. The letters that she had received did not explain that although she wasn't a named tenant, she had the right to talk to the council as an interested party.

Issues around communication were compounded by the difficulties faced by prisoners, due to the nature of their confinement, to communicate with outside agencies. Interviewee G described the barriers in place to contacting his SPAN worker: having to write down a telephone number then wait a week before being allowed to make a phone call, or being questioned when taking a letter to the hall. Other interviewees mentioned letters going missing or being delayed in being delivered.

4. Supporting Prisoners; Advice Network (SPAN) Scotland

This section provides an overview of the SPAN service, what it does and how people accessed the service.

SPAN is a project established for both prisoners and their families to prevent homelessness. It offers independent advice and support to people with convictions at all stages of the journey into, within and upon leaving prison.

Shelter Scotland provides advice and advocacy on all areas of housing in HMP Grampian and HMP Perth, Inverness CAB provide advice and advocacy on all areas of housing in HMP

Inverness and Sacro provides throughcare support within the community post liberation.

Throughout the interviews conducted to inform this report, there was general reference to SPAN's work and how the service had helped in relation to the particular issues raised.[35] In addition, we asked interviewees two specific questions around their interaction with the SPAN project:[36]

- 'How has SPAN/ Shelter Scotland worked with you?', and
- 'What do you think would have happened if you weren't involved with SPAN/ Shelter Scotland?'

Accessing the SPAN service

The Link Centre within each prison has the potential to be the meaningful route to SPAN services due to the core screening process completed by prison staff at the point of entry into prison. This provides an opportunity for housing issues to be identified as soon as possible and so that SPAN can advocate to prevent loss of a tenancy. In reality, this route was the (selfstated) referral route for only 5 of our interviewees. Three interviewees commented on the fact that the screening was not the most appropriate place to do this due to the proximity to the start of their sentence (K, P), and the highly emotional and stressful point at which it takes place (N). The environment and situation were not seen to be conducive to a frank discussion about other areas of life affected by imprisonment.

Other referral routes included:

- Fellow inmates (B, F, K, M).
- Referrals to SPAN through other agencies working both internally (N, P) and externally to the prison (I, J).
- Self-referral (D, G, O). This of course relies on prisoners knowing a) that they need help, and b) how to get it: " you have to be very proactive and keep on at them [the prison officers] until they link you…if it wasn't for me and my big mouth… " (G).

- Interviewee K commented that the process and structure for sharing information about services needed to be improved, for example making more leaflets available.
- Proactive contact by SPAN staff, for prisoners who were in prison for the second or subsequent time (C, M). This information sharing was important in enabling SPAN to respond quickly to risk of homelessness and therefore increasing the chance of successful prevention.

What SPAN does

Practical solutions

For many of the interviewees the first and most basic step that SPAN took was to ensure that the landlord knew that the tenancy was not abandoned, " I don't think [housing association] would have heard from me if it wasn't for SPAN " (A). In three cases covered in the interviews SPAN was investigating a 'qualifying occupier', sub-let or joint tenancy, or had negotiated this already. For some, however, due to the length of their sentence and without anyone being available to take the tenancy on in their absence, closing down the tenancy is the only viable option. For interviewee M, SPAN assisted them to do this in a constructive way, so as not to accrue rent arrears and to explore recovering possessions.[37] In total in 2014, SPAN worked with 467 service users. 64% of these (299) had a tenancy when they entered prison and of these, 84% (250) were successfully supported to keep this tenancy upon release. (See Appendix B for more SPAN statistics).

Negotiating with landlords

A large proportion of the work that SPAN staff had undertaken to prevent tenancies ending was through negotiating with landlords on a case by case basis. For example, SPAN staff:

- Asserted that the service user had a high likelihood of receiving a Home Detention Curfew (commonly known

as a tag) in the near future, so would resume paying rent shortly (B, D).

- Negotiated that the service user was eligible for succession to the tenancy, after his relative had passed away whilst the service user was in prison (F).
- Challenged a local authority's letter that threatened eviction yet did not state any legal grounds (K.)
- Reasoned that the service user (H) had a local connection to the area as he was an employee of the local authority, despite a previous decision that no connection existed and therefore the service user wasn't eligible for homelessness assistance in that area.

Paying the rent

The main reason for people being evicted during their time in custody is the accrual of rent arrears, which for some interviewees had started before going into prison.

Provision is made by the Department for Work and Pensions (DWP) for Housing Benefit to be paid to prisoners in certain circumstances. However, due to challenges with paperwork and communication, this is not always claimed or received as it should be.

In almost every case, SPAN had worked with the DWP to ensure that the Housing Benefit that should be paid during custody was in place. In addition, there were several strategies SPAN employed to tackle rent arrears for the interview cases. For example, SPAN staff:

- Demonstrated two interviewees (D, P) were due Housing Benefit for periods prior to going into custody, secured the backdating of these payments and used these to negotiate with and placate the landlord and retain the tenancy.
- Organised contributions to rent arrears by family members or by the service user themselves, for example one service user sent some of their prison pay through a credit union (O).

- Arranged payments plans to be put in place for some interviewees when they were liberated, and organized appointments to ensure that full Housing Benefit could be reinstated as soon as possible after liberation.
- Organised discretionary housing payments for two interviewees subject to the removal of the spare room subsidy to cover the shortfall, alongside helping them to make sensible decisions about downsizing in the future to more affordable homes (D,F).
- Considered whether bankruptcy was appropriate for one service user (G) whose debt was so large that a repayment plan would not be appropriate.

Engaging with the courts

In cases where landlords had commenced court eviction proceedings, SPAN was fully engaged in the process in order to save the tenancy, for example, through recalling decrees where it is possible and appropriate to do so (F). If a case goes to court, where possible SPAN would provide a defense lawyer, through Shelter Scotland's own legal team if feasible. For example for interviewee G, a decree for eviction was recalled and the case was made that the tenancy was reinstated whilst under recall, providing an address for a tag to be assigned to and as such enabled the tag to be issued.

Ongoing support to settle in a home

Although charting the support needs of participants was beyond the scope of the current study, there are multiple, robust studies that have shown the high prevalence of multiple support needs among prison leavers.[38] Evidence from the literature suggests that ensuring tenancy sustainment for prison leavers requires holistic assessment identifying the full range of housing related and wider support needs,[39] and that if practical needs remain unmet, progress in reforming behaviour and other areas of development are unlikely to be successful.[40]

Six interviewees mentioned that they had appreciated the holistic practical support that exists alongside housing advice within SPAN, including accessing funding to pay off arrears on utility bills (for example C), and one interviewee who highlighted his need for support in sourcing a bed (E). Three others talked about having ongoing support from staff that they had found helpful in the process of leaving the prison and resettling into the community, such as in looking for opportunities for meaningful activity (D, H, M).

Contacting and supporting relatives

SPAN doesn't solely support prisoners, but also their families. In Scotland, imprisonment affects an estimated 16,500 children annually.[41] Two interviewees noted that SPAN had been in touch with their partners to make sure that everyone was informed of what was happening and to progress their case (A, N). One example of family support was work with the ex-partner of someone who was in custody, who had become homeless with her young son due to her ex-boyfriend's conviction and eviction (J). SPAN assisted the service user with her homelessness application and in navigating the temporary accommodation process.

How SPAN works

A theme also emerged through the discussions around the ways in which the team had worked with the interviewees, with comments regarding the reassurance and information provided by SPAN, as well as the proactive and integrated approach taken.

The process of having somebody listen to concerns, understand their situation and act in their interests had lifted the sense of anxiety for interviewees (L, O);

> "The main thing was reassurance that I wasn't losing my house"(G)

> "[SPAN] will really fight your corner " (M, N).

In contrast to the strong sense of "not knowing" some interviewees described with regards to certain systems and processes in the prison, three interviewees commented on the clear communication from SPAN staff (D, J, L).

The proactive design of the SPAN service was highlighted in the interviews – " She's done a lot – she went a bit further than I'd asked her to do " (P). A clear example of this was SPAN staff looking at lists of people entering the prison and proactively arranging meetings with previous service users, allowing them to work quickly to prevent the loss of a tenancy without having to go through the usual prison referral process.

Eight of the interviewees spoke positively about the integrated way that SPAN works with other agencies to help them, such as in one case requesting information from the police to challenge an intentionality decision for a homelessness application (J). Another mentioned the way in which SPAN workers had sought and found the right person from the council/ housing association to talk to directly about their tenancy and had negotiated successfully with them. " Shelter will work together with other services. They ken me on a personal level and pass it on. " (N). In addition, the importance of continuity of support after liberation was highlighted. Both these themes are supported by existing research and literature on this topic.[42, 43, 44]

5. Conclusion

The 16 interviews with SPAN service users gave a valuable, and often poignant, insight into their experiences around housing. Interviewees shared their high levels of anxiety, fear of being released to accommodation that would set them back again and their overwhelming sense of being at the mercy of systems they don't understand.

The general assumption amongst prisoners had been that they would become homeless. Many of the people we spoke to had received letters from their landlords suggesting that they give up their tenancy and some had been threatened with eviction, on

occasion without due reason. Others felt so intimidated by the mounting rent arrears that they felt hopeless.

Perhaps most powerfully, we heard about how much having a home matters to people who have spent time in custody. A home meant far more than just accommodation for the people we spoke to: it represented a sanctuary, something to have pride in and safety for the future. Crucially, we received the strong message from interviewees that they believed having a home would reduce the chance that they would reoffend. Almost all of our interviewees believed that they would have become homeless if they had not received help.

The housing pathways of interviewees showed definitively that it was possible to keep their home during time in custody and, thus, to be prevented from becoming homeless. SPAN staff had saved many tenancies using a wide range of skills and tools. The service that interviewees had received went well beyond traditional housing advice, with proactive, practical help being offered both in prison and postliberation. Often this had included intensive negotiation with landlords, linking with family members or getting involved with finances to put together payment plans. That staff had been reassuring, informing and proactive was also important for interviewees, alongside the integrated nature of the service with other agencies.

Behind the individual stories we observed systems and processes that do not help – and in some cases positively hinder – prisoners' housing pathways. The most fundamental challenge is the lack of priority across a number of partners given to housing need which, as the interviews highlighted, is the goal for successful community reintegration and desistance. The recommendations section to follow details where improvements can be made, how and by whom, to ensure that fewer prisoners are released into homelessness and an increased risk of reoffending.

6. Recommendations

The following recommendations draw on what we heard from the interviewees, combined with Shelter Scotland's longer policy and practice experience in this area. The recommendations are divided between strategic issues and the promotion of good practice on the ground.

To see real change effected in the reduction of reoffending it is crucial that both strategic frameworks and practical implementation prioritise the prevention of homelessness for prisoners.

Strategic Recommendations

This report highlights several themes which are integral to the evolving Community Justice agenda. The Community Justice (Scotland) Bill (in draft at the time of writing) has set out its plans for a national strategy and performance framework with devolved accountability at a local level. This provides an excellent opportunity to stitch housing into the fabric of any discussions around recidivism. However, there are specific points that should be addressed in the establishment or delivery of Community Justice Scotland and the new community justice partnerships in order to bring about effective positive change.[45]

Housing given central place in community justice agenda

> "It's over a year and a half since I've been in a home… I want somewhere I can call mine " (H)

At every level of community justice, stable housing needs to be acknowledged as crucial to desistence, providing a foundation for successful re-integration. A house is a home for those who have been in prison in the same way as it is for everyone else. The emerging themes of home as a source of pride and community support, as well as a place of safety, reflects a basic human need without which we all struggle.

RECOMMENDATION 1: Stable housing should be given due recognition as a foundation of desistance in the national Community Justice Strategy. This should be reflected in national

outcomes performance framework targets being set around sustainment of tenancies and positive housing outcomes to ensure consistency of provision across Scotland.

A national network of housing advice

The experience of Shelter Scotland services is that the currently piecemeal provision of housing advice for prisoners and lack of knowledge about geographically distant housing options does not correlate with the frequent movement of prisoners around the prison estate. Nationally networked services are needed that can provide specialist localised advice and support to proactively maintain tenancies and prevent homelessness, but also provides close links and integrated knowledge with receiving authorities across Scotland.

RECOMMENDATION 2: As a national body, Community Justice Scotland in partnership with the Scottish Prisons Service should consider investigating how housing advice could be best delivered across Scotland to ensure that prisoners that are incarcerated at a distance from the area they will return to receive the same level of service as prisoners that are returning to the local area.

Prison officer training

"Some of the prison officers don't know how it works with housing... some of them don't care " (G)

As the most frequent point of contact during someone's time in custody, prison officers should be aware of the basic issues around housing, its importance in the rehabilitation of offenders and the specialist agencies that are available to provide advice and support in the prison.

RECOMMENDATION 3: Basic, advanced and refresher training on housing issues should be included in the training offered by Community Justice Scotland through its hub function, as well as ensuring that local knowledge about agencies delivering housing advice and support working in local areas is also shared.

Resources

> "People who haven't got a house and are isolated, when they're going to leave, they say, like, 'I'll do a crime and be back next week' " (P)

The evidence from the interviews adds weight to the already well-established case for the effectiveness of prevention and the 'spend-to-save' approach. The cost of not providing effective housing advice and support is wide and falls to many parties. For example, agitated prisoners require more supervision from prison officers, eviction costs for landlords and homelessness processes provided by the local authority. Most significantly, however, is the increased likelihood of reoffending, which carries substantial financial costs, as well as costs to society. Financial resources must be made available for preventative services that secure positive housing outcomes for prisoners on release.

RECOMMENDATION 4: A proportion of the funding received by the Community Justice Partners should be dedicated to improving the housing advice and support available to prisoners.

Good Practice Recommendations

From the themes drawn out in the interviews and the direct voice of SPAN service users themselves we identified specific ways of working as being particularly effective in preventing homelessness and appreciated by service users. Community Justice Scotland may wish to consider these recommendations as part of its remit around learning and development.

Housing advice is intensive, proactive and creative

> "She really fought my corner " (M)

The work of SPAN in providing housing advice went far beyond traditional models of housing advice. Staff had helped prisoners to keep their home by working proactively and creatively with landlords and a range of other agencies to sustain a tenancy until release. For prisoners that had not been able to keep their home, SPAN worked with them to access a home by discussing housing

options and by working with landlords to help secure a tenancy and support resettlement.

RECOMMENDATION 5: Service commissioners should allow capacity in service design and funding for housing advice teams to carry out more intensive work, which takes time but is more effective in preventing homelessness and reducing offending in the long run.

Involve families

"Without them I'd be stuck " (O).

Relatives were often found to be a source of practical help and could be instrumental in saving tenancies. These networks of support are a valuable resource that, with time and effort, can be mobilised to help prevent homelessness.

RECOMMENDATION 6: Where possible, community justice practitioners should investigate whether relatives could help to prevent the end of tenancy e.g. through payment of rent, collection of mail, paying bills, checking security of property etc.

Belongings

"I would have lost my house and everything in it…the important things…photos of my bairns " (D)

The loss of identification, valuables and items of sentimental value can set someone's resettlement back post-release. Ways need to be found for prisoners' belongings to be kept safely if they have to lose their tenancy.

RECOMMENDATION 7: Registered Social Landlords and community justice practitioners or supportive relatives should work together to facilitate a trusted person collecting specific personal items before a tenancy is closed down. SFHA/ALACHO should consider issuing a briefing note on the impact of disposal of belongings for prisoners and should point members towards best practice solutions.

Resettlement location

"It's got to be the right move " (F)

The location of a tenancy is important for people postrelease from prison: evidence shows that positive and negative social influences can be significant determinates of the risk of reoffending. Currently, local allocation policies can work in opposition to prison leavers accessing accommodation that will promote desistance. It is essential that the person leaving prison is involved in the decisions around where they are best placed to live.

One alternative to the allocation restrictions of socially rented housing is the private rented sector, which can provide a means for prisoners to access housing options in geographical areas that would be helpful for them. However, there are significant access issues for prison leavers including affordability and the need for a deposit.

RECOMMENDATION 8: When considering a homeless application from a prison leaver, local authority staff should consider applicants that would not usually be considered to have a local connection as a 'special circumstance',[46] understanding that they are likely to have a 'good reason'[47] for applying to that area.

RECOMMENDATION 9: Local authority private rented sector access schemes should be open to prison leavers and include a rent deposit guarantee scheme.[48] The importance of private rented sector access schemes, especially for prison leavers, should be mentioned in the Housing Options Guidance currently being developed for Scotland.

Avoid hostels

"I'd have went back to hostels, got drinking, been back [in prison] again quick " (M)

Often individuals are placed in hostels as emergency accommodation because they have not been able to make a homelessness application prior to release, so there has not been time to plan more appropriate accommodation (see recommendation below). Interviewees for this research strongly held that being placed in hostels as temporary accommodation would have a negative impact on their reoffending and wellbeing. The cycle

of prison – hostel – prison is well documented and the risk of substance misuse relapse creates anxiety for people leaving prison.

RECOMMENDATION 10: Wherever possible, local authority homelessness teams should avoid placing prison leavers in hostels as temporary accommodation.

Early intervention

"Sometimes by the time you get seen your house is gone " (P)

Advice and support around housing issues should be available as soon as possible once someone enters custody, in order to have the best chance of saving an existing tenancy. However, questions about someone's housing situation will not always be fully or accurately responded to during the core screening process. If a prisoner identifies that they will be homeless on release, a homelessness application should be made as soon as possible in order that appropriate temporary accommodation can be planned.

RECOMMENDATION 11: Prisoners who have tenancies should be proactively asked on multiple occasions by key prison officers (who have been trained to understand basic housing issues) as a matter of routine about their housing situation.

RECOMMENDATION 12: Prison staff and local authority homelessness teams should partner to form protocols, as exist in many areas already, to ensure that homelessness assessments are being carried out prior to release so that alternative forms of temporary accommodation can be planned. This should be monitored by community justice partnerships, and incorporated into Housing Options Guidance.

Proactive promotion

"The amount of people in halls that d'nae ken where they are wi' their hoose " (F)

Proactive promotion to prisoners of potential housing issues and the services that are available to assist will increase awareness and help people to address issues as soon as possible. Homelessness for many could be avoided if prisoners were made more aware

of the circumstances in which they might have need for help with housing.

RECOMMENDATION 13: Scottish Prisons Service should encourage proactive promotion across the prison estate through best practice materials being identified, modified and shared across all prisons (e.g. posters, videos, leaflets, sessions at induction etc.).

Landlord communication

"It was a mandate letter or something like that saying if I fill this in if I want to give my hoose up, and I started panicking " (A)

A lot of stress and unnecessary homelessness could be avoided if landlords communicated clearly and appropriately with people in custody about their tenancy rights, responsibilities and the help that might be available to them.

RECOMMENDATION 14: The Scottish Housing Regulator should monitor communication to tenants that are in custody as part of the Landlord's responsibility under Section 2 of the Scottish Social Housing Charter.

Endnotes

1. Scottish Government, Operation of the Homeless Persons Legislation in Scotland: 2014/15 http://www.gov.scot/Topics/Statistics/Browse/HousingRegeneration/RefTables
2. Niven S and Stewart D (2005) Resettlement outcomes on release from prison, Home Office Findings 248 http://webarchive.nationalarchives.gov. uk/20110314171826/http://rds.homeoffice.gov.uk/rds/pdfs05/r248.pdf
3. Cited Reid Howie, 2004
4. Social Exclusion Unit (2002) Reducing Reoffending by Ex-Prisoners
5. Scottish Government's latest available statistics: http://www.gov.scot/Publications/2012/06/6972/13
6. Loucks, N (2007) Housing Needs of offenders and ex-offenders, Glasgow: The Robertson Trust. Page 4, Section 1
7. 49% of prisoners surveyed said that they had lost their tenancy/accommodation when they went into prison. Scottish Prison Service (2013) Prisoner Survey 2013, Edinburgh: SPS
8. E.g. Homeless Link (2011) Better Together: Preventing Reoffending and Homelessness
9. E.g. McHardy, Fiona (2010) Out of Jail But Still Not Free: Experiences of temporary accommodation on leaving prison, EPIC/ The Poverty Alliance
10. In Glasgow in 1999, 44% of people living in hostels or sleeping rough had been in prison at least once. Homelessness Task Force (2002) Homelessness: An Action Plan for the Prevention and Effective Response. Report from the Homelessness Task Force to Scottish Ministers, Edinburgh: Scottish Executive 11. The Social Exclusion Unit found a reduction in recidivism of 20% for those who had stable accommodation compared to those who didn't. Social Exclusion Unit (2002) Reducing Reoffending by Ex-Prisoners

12. The 'Surveying Prisoner Crime Reduction' survey found that 11% respondents who had served a previous sentence were sleeping rough prior to custody, compared to 3% who had not been in prison before. Williams K, Poyser J, and Hopkins K (2012) Accommodation, homelessness and reoffending of prisoners: Results from the Surveying Prisoner Crime Reduction (SPCR) survey, Ministry of Justice

13. Homelessness Task Force (2002) Homelessness: An Action Plan for the Prevention and Effective Response. Report from the Homelessness Task Force to Scottish Ministers, Edinburgh: Scottish Executive 14. Scottish Government and COSLA (2009) Prevention of Homelessness Guidance

15. Scottish Executive (2006) National Strategy for the Management of Offenders

16. Christie (2011) Commission on the Future Delivery of Public Services

17. Scottish Government, Operation of the Homeless Persons Legislation in Scotland: 2014/15 http://www.gov.scot/Topics/Statistics/Browse/HousingRegeneration/RefTables

18. Niven S and Stewart D (2005) Resettlement outcomes on release from prison, Home Office Findings 248 http://webarchive.nationalarchives.gov. uk/20110314171826/http:// rds.homeoffice.gov.uk/rds/pdfs05/r248.pdf

19. E.g. Reid Howie (2004) The Provision of Housing Advice to Prisoners in Scotland: An evaluation of the projects funded by the Rough Sleepers Initiative. Edinburgh: Scottish Executive Social Research and Loucks, N (2007) Housing Needs of Offenders and Ex-Offenders, Glasgow: The Robertson Trust

20. McHardy, F (2010) Out of jail but still not free: Experiences of temporary accommodation on leaving prison. Glasgow: EPIC/ The Poverty Alliance

21. Tabner, K (2013) Developing positive social networks: Research into the application and effects of a networks approach to homelessness. Edinburgh, Rock Trust

22. Williams et al (2012) Accommodation, homelessness and reoffending of prisoners: Results from the Surveying Prisoner Crime Reduction (SPCR) survey, Ministry of Justice Research Summary 3/12, London: Ministry of Justice

23. Social Exclusion Unit (2002) Reducing Offending by ex-prisoners, London: Social Exclusion Unit

24. Andrews, D and Bonta, J (2003) The Psychology of Criminal Conduct (3rd edition). Cincinnati: Anderson Publishing

25. Loucks, N (2007) Housing Needs of Offenders and Ex-Offenders, Glasgow: The Robertson Trust

26. Scottish Prison Service Corporate Plan 2014-2017: Unlocking potential – transforming lives, Edinburgh: SPS

27. This trend of offenders leaving prison and going into hostels is demonstrated by the fact that 30% of all SPAN service users supported in 2014 moved into temporary accommodation or a hostel on release – See Appendix B for a full breakdown of SPAN service user data from 2014

28. For example, Carlisle, J (1996) The housing needs of ex-prisoners, Housing Research 178, York: Joseph Rowntree Foundation

29. Homelessness Task Force (2002) Homelessness: An Action plan for prevention and effective response. Edinburgh, Scottish Executive

30. Sapouna et al (2011) What works to reduce reoffending: A summary of the evidence, Edinburgh: Justice Analytical Services, Scottish Government

31. E.g. James et al. (2004) Just Surviving: The housing and support needs of people on the fringes of homelessness and/ or the criminal justice system in West Yorkshire. Leeds: Leeds Supporting People Team

32. This issue has also been recently highlighted by Anderson et al (2014) Evaluation of the Community Reintegration Project, Social Research, Crime and Justice Research Findings 50/2014. Edinburgh: Scottish Government
33. More information about the SPAN project can be found in Appendix B 34. N.B. Due to the informal nature of the interviews, sometimes these questions were answered in discussion during another part of the interview
35. With the upcoming implementation of the Housing (Scotland) Act 2014, it will become increasingly important for tenancies not to be 'abandoned', which can suspend their eligibility for social housing
36. E.g. Reid Howie (2004) The Provision of Housing Advice to Prisoners in Scotland: An evaluation of the projects funded by the Rough Sleepers Initiative. Edinburgh: Scottish Executive Social Research and Auditor General and Accounts Commission (2011) An Overview of Scotland's Criminal Justice System. Edinburgh, Audit Scotland
37. Auditor General and Accounts Commission (2011) An Overview of Scotland's Criminal Justice System. Edinburgh: Audit Scotland
38. Malloch et al (2013) The elements of effective through- care part 1: International review. Glasgow: Scottish centre for Crime and Justice Research
39. Families Outside (2009) Support and information for children affected by imprisonment, In Brief 4, Edinburgh: Families Outside
40. For example, in prisons which reported partnership arrangements with housing providers, prisoners were less anxious about their prospects on release. Gojkovic et al (2012) Accommodation for ex-offenders: Third sector housing advice and provision. Southampton: Third Sector Research Centre.
41. When relationships between statutory and third sector agencies are strong there is more effective and consistent support for service users. Malloch et al (2013) The elements of effective through- care part 1: International review. Glasgow: Scottish centre for Crime and Justice Research
42. Continuity of support, in the development of trusted relationships, is a core element of successful continuing engagement Malloch et al (2013) The elements of effective through-care part 1: International review. Glasgow: Scottish centre for Crime and Justice Research
43. The implementation of these changes is still a few years away. In the meantime, recommendations made to Community Justice Partnerships are equally as applicable to the current Community Justice Authorities in the transition period.
44. Scottish Executive (2005) Homelessness Code of Guidance, Section 8.16
45. Scottish Executive (2005) Homelessness Code of Guidance, Section 8.2
46. As included in England's 'Gold Standard Challenge' for Housing Options
47. Social Exclusion Unit (2002) Reducing Reoffending by Ex-Prisoners
48. Scottish Government's latest available statistics: http://www.gov.scot/ Publications/2012/06/6972/13

Repeat Offenders Drive Crime

Robert Matas

Robert Matas is an independent writer who previously spent a 32-year career at the Globe and Mail, as a news and investigative reporter.

E mily Grant was homeless for around six years, often sleeping in back lanes and abandoned cars and spending up to $300 a day to support a heroin and crack cocaine habit.

Like her homeless addicted friends, she raised the money to buy drugs any way she could. Most of her money came from prostitution. Her friends also turned to drug dealing and theft.

Ms. Grant, 28, now lives in an apartment, no longer works as a prostitute and is staying away from narcotics. Some of her friends have also moved off the street and away from crime, a trend reflected in statistics released earlier this week on crime in Vancouver.

Crime rates, driven mostly by addicts looking for money to buy drugs, have dropped significantly in the city over the past five years. Property crime has dropped by 29 per cent since 2007, while violent crime has declined by 12 per cent.

A chronic offender program that includes efforts to providing housing and drug treatment has made a difference, Vancouver Police Chief Jim Chu told the Vancouver Police Board. Ms. Grant echoed his words, saying she believes repeat offenders will not change without measures to deal with their addiction.

Her friends find shoplifting "incredibly easy," she said over a chai at a coffee shop in East Vancouver. Occasionally they are caught, but they just laugh at how police and the courts respond.

One of her friends got a three-month sentence on his sixth offence. He came out of jail and went right back to doing the same

thing. "He had to, to support his [drug habit] He knew no other way," she said.

Without hearing about statistics, Ms. Grant knew from the buzz on the street that break-ins had dropped off. Police in the past few years have been responding to break-ins much faster in Vancouver, making it difficult to flee before the cops arrive, she said.

"I heard people who do them say it is very difficult to do them in Vancouver. You have to go out to the outskirts, like Langley or Abbotsford," she said.

Ms. Grant also knew firsthand what Mayor Gregor Robertson says – that providing decent housing to the homeless can be a step toward reducing crime. Ms. Grant got her apartment through At Home/Chez Soi , a national, $110-million project on mental health and homelessness.

"It's a one-bedroom with a full bathroom and full kitchen, a dishwasher, a garburator. I have large closet space, it's just like a regular apartment," she said. "This … is just so amazing. It is helping so many people, and everything else blossoms from there."

Chief Chu sat next to Mr. Robertson at the police board meeting earlier this week. He appeared pleased to hear board members praise the work of the department based on the most recent crime statistics.

The Canadian Centre for Justice Statistics has reported that Canada's crime rate is at its lowest since the early 1970s. But B.C. has one of the highest crime rates, with 8,404 incidents per 100,000 people, almost double that of Ontario and Quebec. The national average is 6,145 incidents per 100,000 people. Vancouver remains more dangerous than other major Canadian cities.

However, crime rates in Vancouver have dropped significantly over the past five years. The rate of property crime has decreased for nine consecutive years, declining last year to about half the rate of 2002. In the last three months of 2011, property crime decreased by 4.5 per cent citywide. In the southeast corner, property crime dropped by almost 15 per cent.

Violent crimes – homicide, attempted murder, sexual offences, assaults and robberies – are not disappearing as quickly. The rate of violent crime fluctuated in the early part of the past decade before it dropped 12 per cent in the past five years. The rate of sexual offences increased from 2007 to 2010, but dropped by 10 per cent in 2011.

"We're heading in the right direction," Chief Chu told the police board. "The good news is [the crime rate in Vancouver is]dropping faster than any place else in Canada. The not-so-good news is we are still higher than the Canadian average."

Interviews with police, criminologists and the Downtown Vancouver Business Improvement Association turned up several explanations for the significant drop in Vancouver's crime rates: effective policing, changes in society and better housing for the homeless.

Chief Chu talked about the department's chronic offender program that shifts the focus from the crime to the criminal. Detectives prepare extensive biographies of offenders, listing every contact with police, the courts and the penal system. Personal histories, which also include information about an offender's drug addiction and mental health, are sent to Crown counsel and the courts before sentencing, along with victim impact statements and a listing of social services that are available.

When chronic offenders are out of jail, a detective will sit down with them and ask what they need to stay away from crime, Chief Chu said. "We say, what can we do to get you out of this lifestyle – housing, treatment, anything we can do," he said.

Unlike cities with lower numbers, crime rates in Vancouver are driven by repeat offenders who are likely addicted to crack cocaine or crystal meth, and stealing to get their fix, Chief Chu said after the board meeting.

Vancouver has more of those individuals than anywhere else in Canada. They sell stolen goods for 10 cents on the dollar. "Add up how much they have to steal in order to feed that drug habit,"

he said. "When we take a chronic offender off the street, we can see a noticeable reduction in crime," Chief Chu said.

At Home/Chez Soiis a five-year experiment in five cities sponsored by the Mental Health Commission of Canada. The project in Vancouver is looking at what needs to be done to help homeless people who are coping with a drug addiction and mental health issues.

It provides housing first. Once a relationship has been established, the homeless are offered a range of social services to help with substance abuse and mental health issues. Among the research that is underway is a study on whether housing, and the services that go along with that, have an impact on crime involving homeless people, both as victims or perpetrators. Results are expected by the fall of 2012.

Ms. Grant already knows the answer. "Being inside makes a big difference. ... When you are living on the street, it is so depressing. You want to be constantly high to get away from the horribleness of your reality," she said. "But when you are in a home, it is so much easier to cut your drug use down."

Mr. Grant said she eased off drugs after she moved to her apartment and has been clean for over a year. She is now working on completing Grade 12 and hopes to do a course on drug and alcohol counselling. "I feel ecstatic," she said. "I wake up every morning and I feel thankful that I am indoors."

Homelessness Is the Crime in Some Places

Michael Maskin

Michael Maskin studied American Studies and Political Science at Tufts University in Medford, MA, and also served as the Tisch Summer Fellow at the National Law Center on Homelessness and Poverty in Washington, DC.

Tonight, thousands of homeless people in the United States will face the possibility of arrest because they do not have a safe place to sleep. Thousands more could be arraigned for sitting or standing in the wrong place. While they must sleep rest their legs, homeless people live in cities where these and other life sustaining activities are against the law, even though shelters face a critical shortage of beds.

Criminalization laws can take many forms. Most commonly, they outlaw sitting, sleeping in vehicles or outdoors, lying down, "hanging out," sharing food, and camping. What makes them even more insidious is that they can be difficult to detect. Curfews on public parks are often explained by municipalities as a way to deter drug-related crimes. In reality, they are frequently a way to ensure that homeless people don't use park benches as beds. By not having enough safe sleeping spaces, cities are forcing their homeless persons to live on the streets with virtually no other options, and then arresting them for doing so. These laws represent a gross violation of human rights, and have received a large amount of criticism from civil rights advocates around the country and the world.

In March, criminalization laws led to a man's death. 56-year-old Jerome Murdough, a homeless veteran, was without shelter in New York City on a cold night. Searching for a safe place to sleep, he took refuge in an enclosed stairwell in a Harlem public housing

"No Safe Place: How Cities Are Making It Illegal to be Homeless," by Michael Maskin, Center for American Progress, August 11, 2014. Reprinted by permission.

building. He was discovered and arrested for trespassing. Since he didn't have $2,500 to post bail, he was sent to Riker's Island Prison, where he was placed in a hot cell and ignored for hours by prison staff. According to a city official, Murdough "basically baked to death" in the cell, and was found dead on the floor. His disturbing saga highlights the dangers of criminalization laws; instead of receiving needed assistance, Murdough was treated like a criminal, and ultimately lost his life by trying to protect it.

The National Law Center on Homelessness and Poverty recently released a report entitled, No Safe Place: The Criminalization of Homelessness in U.S. Cities. The report details the alarming upward trend of these inhumane and ineffective statutes that criminalize homelessness—with specific examples from around the country—and highlights how the laws are both ineffective and also violations of human rights.

While Murdough's death represents the most extreme effect of criminalization laws, countless other homeless people face situations every day that put their lives in danger. In No Safe Place, the Law Center recounts the story of Lawrence Lee Smith, a man in Boise, Idaho who became homeless after a degenerative joint disease made him unable to continue to work construction.

"He lived in a camper van for years until it was towed. He couldn't afford to retrieve it, leaving him with nowhere to reside but in public places…due to frequent overcrowding of area homeless shelters. Mr. Smith was cited for illegal camping and was jailed for a total of 100 days. Due to the arrest, he lost his tent, his stove, and the fishing equipment he relied upon to live."

In addition to a loss of property, many homeless people who are cited for sleeping in public also must pay fines that they can't afford, which often results in jail time. A homeless woman, Sandy, tells her story in the report:

"I just basically wanted to get in a little bit safer situation so I hid . . . in this church. And they gave me a ticket and now I can't pay for this ticket; it's four-hundred bucks! You know, I can't pay $80 dollars. I have no income whatsoever."

In some cities, it is illegal to share food with homeless people. The report details the case of Birmingham, Alabama Pastor Rick Wood, who was ordered by police to stop serving hotdogs and bottled water to homeless people in a city park.

"'This makes me so mad,' Wood told a local news station. 'These people are hungry, they're starving. They need help from people. They can't afford to buy something from a food truck.'"

Bans on food-sharing exist in 17 of the cities studied by the Law Center and are based on the wrong assumption that free food services will bring an influx of homeless persons to the area. In reality, the bans simply force people to search for food in less safe places like dumpsters and trash cans.

There has been a nationwide increase in criminalization laws since 2011, despite mounting evidence that criminalization is the most expensive and least effective way to deal with homelessness. As cities increasingly opt for these bad policies, there will eventually be no safe place left for homeless people. Instead, communities should focus on constructive alternatives to criminalization that actually work; policies like the "housing first" strategy that provides housing and supportive services to homeless people and is also much less costly than the price of jail stays and emergency room visits.

Could you survive if there were no place you were allowed to fall asleep, store your belongings, or stand still? There are far better policy choices than criminalization and making it illegal for people to simply try to survive; policies that are better for homeless people, and better for the character of our nation.

The Homeless Aren't Any More Likely to Commit Crime

Domenic Poli

Domenic Poli, a University of Massachusetts graduate, has spent the last seven years as a news reporter for The Brattleboro Reformer, a Vermont based news website.

There are people who tend to associate the homeless with poor life decisions, high crime rates, and disturbance calls to the police. But local law enforcement officers and health professionals say there is little to no correlation between a person's living situation and the commission of crime.

Capt. Mark Carignan, of the Brattleboro Police Department, said the police come into contact with the homeless under a variety of circumstances — such as complaints from the public or simple welfare checks — but he sees no evidence that suggests someone without a home is more likely to engage in criminal activity.

"I can say we do not experience a higher commission of crime among the homeless. Though, we might deal with homeless people more often (than with other demographics)," he said. "It's not unusual to get calls from people about someone drinking alcohol in public or just hanging around in public and citizens will call and say someone is drinking or is intoxicated on a park bench and we'll go down and talk with them."

Carignan said when officers handle a situation involving a homeless person, their mission isn't so much enforcement-minded as it is about getting that person to a place where they may be a little safer. He said just issuing tickets and sending people on their way might treat a symptom, but it does not address any problem.

Carignan mentioned, however, enforcement measures will be taken if more hospitable methods are ineffective on repeat offenders.

The captain also said a social worker, Kristen Neuf, who is a Health Care & Rehabilitation Services of Vermont employee, works regularly with the department and officers will often bring her along when there is a case involving a homeless person.

"It's been very beneficial," he said. "That program has been a significant asset to the police department and to the community. It enables us to provide better service to the community and frees up patrol officers."

Carignan said there are several resources for the homeless throughout Brattleboro, such as Morningside Shelter and the Brattleboro Area Drop In Center, and police officers do their best to refer people to these services.

Lucie Fortier, the executive director at the Drop In Center, told the Reformer the organization works closely with the BPD. She said she calls the department the first night the Winter Overflow Shelter is open every year to remind officers to bring people to the shelter if necessary. She does the same with Rescue Inc. Fortier said the shelter at the First Baptist Church on Main Street opened its doors for the season on Nov. 2 and was the first in the state to do so.

She said the shelter, which is entering its eighth year of operation, is scheduled to close on April 15, but remained open until May 1 last year. Fortier mentioned the shelter has hosted 100 unduplicated individuals so far this season. The shelter is open every day from 5 p.m. to 7 a.m.

Fortier also expressed gratitude to the interfaith clergy for making sure hot dinners are provided each night.

Windham County Sheriff Keith Clark said he does not track crime related to the homeless, though he does not believe there is a significant problem. He said the local shelters do a fine job of helping people, but there is still a void that must be filled.

"It's a bed and dinner, but it's got to be more than that. And it's not necessarily asking the state to write another check," Clark said. "Part of it is educating the public."

Clark also mentioned his department gets calls from people looking for a warm place to stay.

"You have to wonder what it's like to live like that in this region," he added.

Hinsdale, N.H., Police Chief Todd Faulkner said the crimes involving the homeless are typically non-violent and out of desperation. He said his department is called to Walmart roughly 600 times a year for numerous reasons and many of those instances involve people shoplifting something they need or trespassing.

"I've arrested people with stolen food from Walmart and from other businesses in town," he said this week.

The chief said homelessness often carries a stigma with it, adding that citizens often call to complain about homeless people holding signs in public places and asking for money.

"They're not really doing anything wrong. They're just looking for food or money," he said. "But it still takes an officer's time."

The chief said homeless people are no more likely to commit a crime than anyone else.

Faulkner also told the Reformer about the case of Paul Hennessey, a Kentucky man who went missing in 2012 and was found by his officers in the old Walmart building at George's Field in Hinsdale. Faulkner said Hennessey was arrested for trespassing and taken to jail (though he would not confirm his identity) and had his fingerprints processed through a database when it was learned he was missing from Kentucky.

"We located his family and it was a great Christmas gift to them. They thought he was dead," the chief said, adding that the family plans to help Hennessey with his mental health issues.

Faulkner also said he will present all the information of the prosecutor's office and there is a possibility Hennessey will not be charged with a crime.

Organizations to Contact

The editors have compiled the following list of organizations concerned with the issues debated in this book. The descriptions are derived from materials provided by the organizations. All have publications or information available for interested readers. This list was compiled on the date of publication of the present volume; the information provided here may change. Be aware that many organizations take several weeks or longer to respond to inquiries, so allow as much time as possible.

Catholic Charities USA

2050 Ballenger Ave. Suite 400, Alexandria, VA 22314
(703) 549-1390
email: info@catholiccharitiesusa.org
website: www.catholiccharitiesusa.org

Catholic Charities USA is a national network of agencies who help the homeless as well as vulnerable people who are in need of help. Of its many services, providing shelter for and feeding the homeless is one of them. Catholic Charities USA was founded in 1910 and is one of the largest U.S. charities.

Center for American Homeless Veterans

210 E. Broad St., Suite 202, Falls Church, VA 22046
(703) 237-8980
email: info@vetsvision.org
website: www.americanhomelessvets.org

The Center for American Homeless Veterans (CAHV) is an advocacy group that educates and supplies the American public with information on the number of homeless veterans. The organization also helps to provide solutions for the vets to adapt themselves back into society after coming home from service.

The CAHV takes a strong stance in making sure that government officials do their part to help our veterans.

Covenant House
461 Eighth Ave., New York, NY 10001
(800) 388-3888
email: tmanning@convenanthouse.org
website: www.covenanthouse.org

The Covenant House was founded in 1972 and is a non-profit that aims to keep children off of the streets. It features Service Center programs in 30 cities in the U.S., Canada, and Central America. In addition to being a charitable organization, the Covenant House also serves as advocates for homeless youth.

National Alliance to End Homelessness
1518 K Street NW, 2nd Floor, Washington, DC 20005
(202) 638-1526
email: info@naeh.org
website: www.endhomelessness.org

Originally formed in 1983 under the name, the National Citizens Committee for Food and Shelter, the National Alliance to End Homelessness switched to its current name in 1987. The organization, now more than 10,000 people strong, is the largest partnership between the people and public agencies in an effort to help end homelessness. The National Alliance to End Homelessness helped decrease homelessness by 10% in the U.S. from 2005-2007.

National Coalition for Homeless Veterans
1730 M Street NW, Suite 705, Washington, DC 20036
(800) 838-4357
email: info@nchv.org
website: www.nchv.org

The National Coalition for Homeless Veterans is a non-profit organization that has a 23-member board of directors. The NCHV serves as a resource center for a network of community-based

service providers around the nation, who provide support services such as housing, food, health services, job training and placement, legal aid, and more to homeless veterans. The organization also helps to serve as an intermediary between care providers, Congress, and executive branch agencies to help all parties with the ultimate goal of ending homelessness for veterans.

National Coalition for the Homeless
2201 P St. NW, Washington, DC 20037
(202) 462-4822
email: info@nationalhomeless.org
website: www.nationalhomeless.org

The National Coalition for the Homeless is a national network of individuals who have experienced homelessness in the past or who are currently battling it. The group has one single mission, which is to end homelessness while making sure that the needs and civil rights of the homeless are protected. The organization has been around for 30 years and also provides numerous research and information guides.

National Law Center on Homelessness & Poverty
2000 M St. NW, Suite 210, Washington, DC 20036
(202) 638-2535
email: email@nlchp.org
website: www.nlchp.org

The National Law Center on Homelessness & Poverty is a Washington, DC non-profit. As the only national legal group that's dedicated to helping put an end to homelessness, the NLCHP was founded in 1989 by Maria Foscarinis, a lawyer who left her firm to dedicate her time to helping the homeless. One of its main goals is to expand access to affordable housing, which will keep more homeless off the streets.

StandUp For Kids

83 Walton St., Suite 500, Atlanta, GA 30303
(800) 365-4543
email: contact@standupforkids.org
website: www.standupforkids.org

StandUp For Kids is a national non-profit charity whose core mission is to end youth homelessness. It teaches kids basic life skills that it hopes will help to keep youth off the streets. Doing this for 27 years, StandUp For Kids had a successful 2016, reuniting 200 runaway or homeless youth with their families.

United States Interagency Council on Homelessness

1275 First St. NE, Suite 227, Washington, DC 20552
(202) 708-4663
email: usich@usich.gov
website: www.usich.gov

The United States Interagency Council on Homelessness was authorized by Congress in 1987. Its main responsibility is to organize the federal response to homelessness and accomplish its goal to end homelessness. The USICH works closely with Cabinet Secretaries and various senior leaders across 19 federal member agencies.

Volunteers of America

1660 Duke St., Alexandria, VA 22314
(703) 341-5000
email: info@voa.org
website: www.voa.org

Volunteers of America is a national non-profit organization in the U.S. that helps people connect with their communities in an effort to help people who need to rebuild their lives. The organization serves the youth, elderly, veterans, homeless, past incarcerated, and the disabled, and helps nearly 2 million people every year. Volunteers of America is made up of 65,000 volunteers across 46 states and has been helping people since 1896.

Bibliography

Books

A.M. Buckley. *Homelessness*. Minneapolis, MN: ABDO Publishing Company, 2011.

Donald W. Burnes. *End Homelessness: Why We Haven't, How We Can*. Boulder, CO: Lynne Rienner Publishers, Inc., 2016.

Kathy Furgang. *Ending Hunger and Homelessness Through Service Learning*. New York, NY: Rosen Publishing Group, 2015.

Noel Merino. *Poverty and Homelessness*. New York, NY: Greenhaven Publishing, 2009.

Kathleen Swenso Miller. *Homelessness in America: Perspectives, Characterizations, and Considerations for Occupational Therapy*. Abingdon, UK: Taylor & Francis, 2007.

Joseph F. Murphy. *Homelessness Comes to School*. Thousand Oaks, CA: SAGE Publications, 2011.

Naomi Nichols. *Youth Work: An Institutional Ethnography of Youth Homelessness*. Toronto, Ontario: University of Toronto Press, 2014.

Diane D. Nilan. *Crossing the Line: Taking Steps to End Homelessness*. St. Petersburg, FL: Booklocker.com, Inc., 2005.

Deborah Padgett. *Housing First: Ending Homelessness, Transforming Systems, and Changing Lives*. New York, NY: Oxford University Press, 2015.

Peter H. Rossi. *Down and Out in America: The Origins of Homelessness*. Chicago, IL: University of Chicago Press, 1989.

Kevin Ryan. *Almost Home: Helping Kids Move from Homelessness to Hope*. New York, NY: Turner Publishing Company, 2012.

Russell K. Schutt. *Homelessness, Housing, and Mental Illness*. Cambridge, MA: Harvard, 2011.

Laura Stivers. *Disrupting Homelessness*. Minneapolis, MN: Augsburg Fortress Publishers, 2011.

Tamara Thompson. *Homelessness*. New York, NY: Greenhaven Publishing, 2011.

Craig Willse. *The Value of Homelessness: Managing Surplus Life in the United States.* Minneapolis, MN: University of Minnesota Press, 2015.

Periodicals and Internet Sources

Emma Brown, "These are the faces of America's growing youth homeless population," *The Washington Post,* June 17, 2016. https://www.washingtonpost.com/news/education/wp/2016/06/17/these-are-the-faces-of-americas-growing-youth-homeless-population/?utm_term=.270b5b3454a7

Miles Bryan, "In Rural America, Homeless Population May Be Bigger Than You Think," *NPR,* February 18, 2016. http://www.npr.org/2016/02/18/467217588/in-rural-america-homeless-population-may-be-bigger-than-you-think

Glenn Ellis, "Number of homeless children and adults in America has increased," *The Philadelphia Tribune,* June 28, 2016. http://www.phillytrib.com/news/health/number-of-homeless-children-and-adults-in-america-has-increased/article_08d18cac-6d3c-55ab-92f1-857321b82252.html

Pam Fessler, "Tide Starts To Turn Against The 'Crime' Of Being Homeless," *NPR,* November 3, 2015. http://www.npr.org/2015/11/03/454249044/tide-starts-to-turn-against-the-crime-of-being-homeless

Thomas L. Friedman, "Homelessness in America," *The New York Times,* November 8, 2016. https://www.nytimes.com/2016/11/09/opinion/were-near-the-breaking-point.html?_r=0

Rick Jervis, "Mental disorders keep thousands of homeless on streets," *USA Today,* August 27, 2014. http://www.usatoday.com/story/news/nation/2014/08/27/mental-health-homeless-series/14255283/

Eric M. Johnson, "More than 500,000 people homeless in the United States: report," *Reuters,* November 19, 2015. http://www.reuters.com/article/us-usa-homelessness-idUSKCN0T908720151120

Xander Landen, "More cities across the U.S. consider homelessness a crime," *PBS,* July 19, 2014. http://www.pbs.org/newshour/rundown/homelessness-now-crime-cities-throughout-u-s/

Christopher Mathias, "There's A Good Reason New York's Homeless Often Sleep In The Subway," *Huffington Post,* October 23, 2015.

http://www.huffingtonpost.com/entry/new-york-homeless-subway_us_56291c1be4b0aac0b8fc0729

Adam Nagourney , "Old and on the Street: The Graying of America's Homeless," *The New York Times*, May 31, 2016. https://www.nytimes.com/2016/05/31/us/americas-aging-homeless-old-and-on-the-street.html

National Law Center on Homelessness & Poverty, "No Safe Place: The Criminalization of Homelessness in U.S. Cities," https://www.nlchp.org/documents/No_Safe_Place

Randeep Ramesh "A fifth of all homeless people have committed a crime to get off the streets," *The Guardian*, December 22, 2010. https://www.theguardian.com/society/2010/dec/23/homeless-committing-crimes-for-shelter

Ben Tracy, "Searching for solutions in America's No. 1 state for homelessness," *CBS News*, November 22, 2016. http://www.cbsnews.com/news/homelessness-rising-in-california-as-communities-search-for-solutions/

Morgan Zalot, "Homelessness in America: HUD Reveals Strides, Setbacks with 2015 Homeless Count Data," *NBC Philadelphia*, November 19, 2015. http://www.nbcphiladelphia.com/news/local/Homelessness-in-America-HUD-Releases-2015-Homeless-Count-Data-351810021.html

Stav Ziv, "Child Homelessness in U.S. Reaches Historic High, Report Says," *Newsweek*, November 17, 2014. http://www.newsweek.com/child-homelessness-us-reaches-historic-high-report-says-285052

Index